USEFUL,
USABLE,
DESIRABLE

Aaron Schmidt *and* Amanda Etches

USEFUL, USABLE, DESIRABLE

APPLYING USER EXPERIENCE DESIGN TO YOUR LIBRARY

An imprint of the American Library Association
Chicago | 2014

Aaron Schmidt has worked as a circulation clerk, young adult librarian, reference librarian, and library director. Currently he is principal of Influx Library User Experience, a design firm dedicated to integrating UX design into libraries. He writes a column in *Library Journal* called "The User Experience," lectures at San José State University's School of Library and Information Science, and serves on the editorial board for *Weave: Journal of Library User Experience*. Schmidt blogs about library design at http://walkingpaper.org.

Amanda Etches is head of Discovery & Access at the University of Guelph Library, where she spends her time guiding teams and projects that are all about making the library experience better for users, both in person and online. She is also part of Influx, a user experience consultancy that works with libraries. Etches has an MA in English Literature and an MISt in Library and Information Science, both from the University of Toronto. She frequently writes and presents on web design, usability, and user experience practices and trends. She tweets @etches and blogs at http://e.tches.ca, two places where you are likely to find her feeling guilty about having so much fun doing exactly what she is supposed to be doing.

© 2014 by the American Library Association

Printed in the United States of America

18 17 16 15 14   5 4 3 2 1

Extensive effort has gone into ensuring the reliability of the information in this book; however, the publisher makes no warranty, express or implied, with respect to the material contained herein.

ISBN: 978-0-8389-1226-3 (paper).

Library of Congress Cataloging-in-Publication Data

Schmidt, Aaron, 1978-
    Useful, usable, desirable : applying user experience design to your library / Aaron Schmidt and Amanda Etches. — First edition.
        pages   cm
    Includes bibliographical references and index.
    ISBN 978-0-8389-1226-3 (alk. paper)
    1. Library administration. 2. Public services (Libraries). 3. Information services—Management. 4. User-centered system design. 5. Library planning. I. Etches, Amanda, 1975- II.Title. III. Title: Improving your library with user experience design.
Z678.S36 2014
025.1—dc23   2014005004

Book design by Kim Thornton in the Chapparal and Trade Gothic typefaces.

♾ This paper meets the requirements of ANSI/NISO Z39.48-1992 (Permanence of Paper).

contents

Chapter 1

Introducing Library User Experience

▶ **WELCOME TO** *USEFUL, USABLE, DESIRABLE: APPLYING USER EXPERIENCE* *Design to Your Library*! We're excited that you're reading this book because we think that user experience (or UX) design is an unparalleled framework for improving and transforming libraries. By designing your library with the user experience in mind, you have the potential to deepen the connection your library has with its community and make your library a place that people love to use. Sounds good, right?

Before we get into the details of how to design a great library user experience, let's unpack this whole *user experience* concept first.

1.1 What Is User Experience Design?

The user experience is how someone feels when using a product or service.

Since most people interact with many different elements of a service or product, there are many different factors that impact someone's overall user experience. Here's an example of all the ways someone might interact with a company to buy a shirt:

- Email from company announcing a new style
- Details on company's website

- Appearance of store's window display
- Signs and store layout
- Music playing in the store
- Customer service
- Product availability
- The fitting room
- The actual shirt

All of these potential places of interaction, these *touchpoints*, would have an impact on the overall experience of buying and wearing this shirt. If this organization is aiming to facilitate an enjoyable experience, it had better pay attention to all of these touchpoints. The goal of user experience design is to manage all these touchpoints so that, together, they provide a great experience.

1.2 Why UX for Libraries?

Libraries might not be in the business of selling shirts, but we do have a lot of different touchpoints to design. And the sum total of someone's experience with a library's touchpoints forms their overall experience—good, bad, or indifferent.

Here's our attempt at an exhaustive list of library touchpoints:

- website
- catalog
- databases
- email
- instant messaging
- text messaging
- online reference
- telephone
- parking lot
- building
- library workers
- signage
- furniture/shelving
- materials
- programs/events/classes
- computers
- brochures/posters
- library card
- print newsletter
- advertisements

If you're feeling some pressure, like there are a lot of library touchpoints and a lot of ways people's experiences can go haywire, you're not alone! The tricky thing about creating an excellent user experience is that everything counts. If your library's services are irrelevant and your building is dirty, outstanding customer service isn't going to be enough to facilitate a good overall user experience. If your building is beautiful but your staff is rude, library members are bound to have a negative experience. The best way to ensure that everyone is primed to have the best experience possible is to optimize all of your library's touchpoints. Don't panic. This book will help you do it. Let's start by talking about the three essential elements of good UX.

1.3 The Trinity of Good UX

Useful. Usable. Desirable. These are the three essential elements required for a great user experience at your library. Let us explain.

Useful
This is the heart of the matter. A product or service must solve a problem or satisfy a need to create a great user experience. If you buy something that's desirable but not useful, a flashy new gadget for instance, you might use it for a while or on occasion, but eventually, it will probably gather dust in a drawer. Clearly this is an important concept for libraries. If we're not useful, we can't be important to our communities.

Usable
What good is something that's useful if it's impossible to use or a constant cause of frustration? Not much good at all. Think here of library databases. They contain some great, useful information but they're often difficult to use. Simply being usable isn't enough to entice people to use our services, but it certainly is essential.

Desirable
In order to really connect with a product or service, people must either need or want to use it (but hopefully both). If your library is providing a service that is both useful and usable, but none of your members want or need that service, you might as well stop providing it.

The thing to remember about the trinity of good UX is that you can't just start by aiming for one of the three elements. Nor can you decide that if your library is routinely hitting two out of three, you're scoring above average, so you're okay. Useful, usable, and desirable are all inextricably linked. Everything you do at your library—every service, every resource, every interface, every space—must satisfy all three elements of good UX, or you're simply not optimizing the experience you could be providing to your members.

Once again, if this notion leaves you feeling overwhelmed, take a deep breath. We're here to help. But before we go any further, before we jump right in and start talking about how to make improvements, we need to discuss some broad concepts. There are eight principles upon which the entire idea of library user experience is predicated. Taken together, these principles are the underlying philosophy of user experience design, and it is only upon these principles that we can build better experiences for our members. Let's explore each of them.

1.4 The Principles of Library User Experience Design

1. You Are Not Your User

The idea that *we are not the people we design things for* comes to us via the world of human-computer interaction and human factors research. In library terms, it simply means that we shouldn't be designing our spaces, services, or interfaces with *ourselves* in mind. Instead, we should be designing those things (and everything else) with *our users* in mind. And we most certainly are not the same as our users because we are library insiders! We know how things are supposed to work, and we bring a baseline of knowledge, experience, and expertise to everything we do that our users don't share. So if we design for ourselves, we're not only putting our users at a distinct disadvantage, we're also pretty much setting them up for failure.

2. The User Is Not Broken

Karen Schneider famously brought this notion to librarian consciousness in 2006 with a manifesto on the very topic of the user not being broken (http://freerange librarian.com/2006/06/03/the-user-is-not-broken-a-meme-masquerading-as-a -manifesto). Once upon a time, the library used to be this thing that we had to teach people how to use. From the card catalog to command-line searching, finding information was shrouded in mystery and only a select few (i.e., librarians) had the key to unlocking the wonders of that mysterious world. If a clueless user sat himself down at a CD-ROM terminal and tried to figure out how to perform a search on his own, a librarian would most certainly intervene because, poor thing, said user wasn't schooled in database searching like we were, so there was no way he could be successful. We remember those days, too, and we miss them about as much as you do (which is to say, not at all). Thankfully, our interfaces aren't designed to be mediated by us anymore, but we still hear librarians making excuses for poorly designed search systems by telling themselves, "We'll just teach them how to use it; then they will be fine." User experience design turns that notion right on its head and says that if someone has to be taught how to use something, then *it's the thing that is broken, not the user*.

3. A Good User Experience Requires Research

It's super easy to sit down with a piece of paper and a pencil and come up with a design for something. Every usability expert's favorite cognitive scientist, Don Norman, uses the example of a bank ATM in many of his presentations and published works (see, e.g., *Emotional Design: Why We Love (or Hate) Everyday Things* [Basic Books, 2003]). When ATMs were first being designed, someone sat down and figured out that all you'd really need is a machine full of cash and a person with a bank card to automate the cash withdrawal process. The cardholder would insert her card into the machine, type in a passcode, tell the machine how much money she wanted, remove the bills from the cash dispensing tray, remove her card, and be on her way. Easy! And perfectly common sense. Except, when ATMs were first built and installed, people often used to take their cash and walk away, forgetting to take their cards, too. If some interaction designer or engineer somewhere didn't stop to watch how people used ATMs, we never would have gotten those new and improved machines that switched up the process, returning your card first before dispensing your cash, thereby reducing the number of left-behind bank cards. By doing that little bit of research, by learning about the lives, preferences, hopes, and dreams of library members, and by learning more about how they use your library, you can adjust your existing services and create better ones.

4. Building a Good User Experience Requires Empathy

If we all did things the way that worked best for us, with no consideration for anyone else, life would certainly be a lot easier for each of us individually, but pretty awful for us as a collective. We mostly don't live that way because of a little thing called empathy. Empathy is all about understanding someone else's feelings and sharing those feelings. Idiomatically, empathy is walking a mile in someone else's shoes. To create meaningful and engaging services that are easy to use, we need to shed our librarian perspectives and think like members. What's more, we have to value this adopted perspective. Only then will we be able to gain the insights we need to create excellent user experiences. One of the best examples we've seen for how to build empathy for our members is "Work Like a Patron Day," an idea started in 2008 by Brian Herzog (www.swissarmylibrarian.net/2008/10/07/work-like-a

-patron-day). The goal is to encourage library staff to experience the library the way library members do, by doing everything from working at public computers to using public washrooms. Activities like these can help us start thinking like members, which is the first step to really gaining empathy for them. The second step—caring about their experiences—cannot be taught and requires careful hiring.

5. A Good User Experience Must Be Easy before It Can Be Interesting

In the world of web development, *easy* before *interesting* usually means functionality before bells and whistles. So when you're designing and building a website, you aim to nail things like site uptime, load speed, and navigation before including things like galleries, home page displays, and user-generated content. Makes sense, right? Well, we believe that those ideas can be easily extrapolated to just about anything that is designed, from spaces to services to service desks themselves.

6. Good User Experience Design Is Universal

Universal design (UD) is a broad concept that aims to produce real-world environments that work just as easily for people with disabilities as they do for people without disabilities. The Center for Universal Design at North Carolina State University has identified seven principles of UD (www.ncsu.edu/ncsu/design/cud/about_ud/udprinciplestext.htm), as follows:

- The design is **equitable** in use to people with diverse abilities.
- The design is **flexible** enough to allow a wide range of individual preferences and abilities.
- The use of the design is **simple and intuitive,** easy to understand regardless of previous experience or skill.
- The design is **perceptible,** such that it communicates information effectively to the user.
- The design is **tolerant of error,** such that it minimizes adverse consequences if used incorrectly.
- The design requires **low physical effort,** allowing use with minimal effort.
- The design accommodates the **size, space, and approach** necessary for use.

We like to call upon these principles when designing in both physical and virtual environments, since they easily map to online accessibility requirements.

7. Good User Experience Design Is Intentional

Try this: walk around your library and ask yourself why things are the way they are. Why is the circulation desk set up the way it is? Why is the reference collection (if you still have one) where it is? Why are the recycling bins where they are? We bet that the answer to most of the questions you ask yourself will be, "Because that's the way it's evolved." Here's a radical notion: everything in your library (physical *and* virtual) should be designed with user behavior in mind; everything in your library should be designed with intent. What does that mean? It means that nothing should be left to chance; nothing should be added or removed or moved or placed "just because"—every aspect of every physical and virtual component of our libraries should be designed the way it is for a specific reason. If that sounds overwhelming or exhausting to you, that's because it is. But trust us when we tell you that it's worth it and that your members will thank you for it.

I'm a designer?

Don't worry. You don't need to wear a black turtleneck and square glasses to be a designer. Whether you like it or not, every time you create a library policy, bookmark, or service, you're making a design decision. Think of design this way: arranging elements to serve a certain purpose. Many design decisions in libraries are what we like to call unintentional design or design by default. This book will get you in the mode of making deliberate decisions. The result will be a better library and happier members. For more about the design process, see chapter 9, section 9.2.

8. Good User Experience Design Is Holistic

We once taught a workshop on UX design to a group of library staff, and as we wrapped up the session, an attendee raised a tentative hand and asked, "How is this different from everything we've always done in libraries? We've always cared about our patrons. We've always been user-centered. We give great customer service!" Ask any library staff member, especially a member of the frontline staff, and we bet they'd say the same thing: we give great customer service. There is a great tendency to boil down UX design to customer service because that's what we know and understand. But good UX design is about so much more than good customer service. Good UX design considers all those touchpoints we mentioned above—not just how your members are treated when they walk into your building, but also how being in that building makes them *feel* and how your building enables them to *accomplish their goals*. For us, this is what a holistic approach to UX design is all about.

Pulse-Check Time

What do you think? Are you on board with these ideas? If you're not, check to make sure you haven't creased the spine of this book and return it now, or head right back to your library and drop it in the book return slot. You won't want to read much more because the rest of this book contains a series of ideas that are all based on these principles, ideas that embody this philosophy. If you *are* on board, great! Read on to find out how these ideas will help you redefine and redesign the user experience at your library.

1.5 How to Use This Book

Each of the central chapters in this book, starting with chapter 3 and ending with chapter 8, deals with a different type of library touchpoint. In each of these chapters, you'll find a brief introduction to the topic and then a series of checkpoints that tackles a specific element of that touchpoint. Each checkpoint will help you

- understand why the topic is important and how it impacts the user experience your library is providing
- assess the experience you're currently providing
- gain an understanding and some ideas for how to make improvements

Each checkpoint also has two types of numbers to deal with: a difficulty rating and a scoring system. Let's make sure you understand each before going any further.

Difficulty Rating

We've employed a really simple system to score each checkpoint to give you a sense of how much time, effort, and skill will likely be involved in getting to optimum performance in that checkpoint. Of course, we're well aware that mileage may vary depending on the library, but we've made some assumptions in order to provide a general guideline. Given our experience, we're pretty confident these generalizations will work for *most* libraries.

Rating	Overview	Scale	Time	Skill
★	A single-starred checkpoint is something that is fairly quick and easy to implement, requiring just a little effort.	**Minor.** Can be completed on the initiative of a single staff-member with no more than department-head approval and minimal budget impact.	A few hours to a week.	No special skills needed.
★ ★	Two-stars indicate that the checkpoint is a bit more involved and will therefore require more time and effort to achieve.	**Moderate.** Might require some financial and organizational support to complete.	One to four weeks.	Some special skills/training may be required to complete this checkpoint.
★ ★ ★	Three-starred items require significant changes on an organizational level and can be accomplished only over a long period.	**Major.** Will require a significant investment at the organizational level, in terms of financial support, cultural change, or both.	Anywhere from a few months to more than a year.	Will likely require extensive skill-development/ training for staff.

Scoring System

The other number in each checkpoint that you'll need to wrap your head around is the scoring system. In order to help you assess the current state of things at your library, each checkpoint includes a section on how to assess and score the experience you're providing in your library. The total score for each chapter is 100, and the score for each checkpoint varies from 10 to 30 points (specific instructions are in each checkpoint).

At the end of the book you'll find an appendix with a list of all the checkpoints. This list serves two purposes: it provides an at-a-glance view of issues surrounding each touchpoint, and it gives you a place to record your scores for each checkpoint. Once you've assessed all of the different checkpoints, you can use the tool at the end of the appendix to give you a graphical overview of the strengths of your library's user experience and where the biggest opportunities for improvement are.

Not interested in keeping score? No problem. While the scoring system is a great tool, using it is optional. If you're not aiming to undertake a bunch of projects right now, you can read this book just to learn about how library touchpoints impact the user experience.

When and Who

There's no reason to use this book in sequential order. If you're embarking on a project to, say, improve your library's website, go straight to chapter 7. That being said, don't ignore any chapters! The more touchpoints you optimize, the more engaging an overall user experience you'll create.

Whether you're a lone UX wolf or part of a more organized effort, you can use this book. If you're just starting off improving UX and your organizational culture is cooperative, we recommend forming a cross-departmental team. Start with some smaller projects that might have a decent impact and build on these early wins.

While we like to advocate for improving your overall user experience in a holistic way, if there's no hope for forming a cross-departmental UX team, you can also use portions of this book that are relevant to your own department. Perhaps if you lead by example other departments will catch on!

1.6 A Note on Terminology

Details are important, and no matter how small it might be, we need to think critically about every aspect of our libraries. One detail overlooked by most libraries is what to call the people who use our institutions.

Most public libraries use *patron* and most academic libraries use *student*. *Student* makes a fair amount of sense to us, but we're not sure why we've settled on *patron*. Is it because people patronize libraries? Or do we use it because it's a holdover from people being patrons of the arts? Either way, this is a legacy term that we use today because we've always used it. We think it's time for a revamp.

User is a common replacement for *patron*—and it's great for general or theoretical discussions about UX and the like, where we rely on the term quite a bit—but when referring to actual people, it's a little impersonal. Plus, it's fraught with implications: users can be people who don't give anything back in return; *user* often refers to someone on drugs (as in "drug user"); *user* is also pretty bland. *User* might make sense to us, but would you ever call someone in your building a *user* to his/her face? Probably not. Why? Because no one wants to be called a *user*.

Then there's *customer*. Though it's often unavoidable—for example, in discussions about *customer* service—we're not fans of the term *customer* because we think it emphasizes a transactional relationship, whereas libraries need to move beyond thinking of interactions with people as transactions. *Customer* is a business term that detracts from the public service element of what we do. We think libraries should not only treat folks with a bit more respect, but we should also label them more accurately.

The best term we've heard is *member*. Not only does the word *member* have few, if any, drawbacks, it is also positive and useful. *Member* evokes a sense of belonging or even ownership. It implies that someone is making an active choice. It indicates that there's an organization in which you can participate and do stuff. Aren't these the things that we should be aiming for? We know of at least one library (Darien Library in Darien, Connecticut) that has already had success using the term, and we think all libraries should follow suit.

Since *member* best describes how we want people using our institutions to feel and act, and since it describes how we think libraries should operate, *member* is the term we will use most often in this book.

Chapter 2

User Research Techniques in This Book

▶ **CENTRAL TO CREATING DELIGHTFUL AND ENGAGING USER EXPERIENCES IS** learning about the needs, preferences, hopes, and dreams of library members. This can be accomplished only through systematic and consistent user research. You'll find some classic user research techniques in this book, but unlike other user experience books or research methodology texts, this one isn't organized according to the techniques. Instead, we've embedded these techniques where we think they will be most useful—where they will help solve problems.

We think user research is important enough to warrant some airtime of its own, so here's a guide to the types of user research we'll cover in this book. For each type of user research method described, we've also included an example of where in the book we've suggested using that research methodology.

2.1 Attitudinal and Behavioral Research

The first important thing to know about user research is that it comes in two varieties: attitudinal research and behavioral research. As the names suggest, attitudinal research uncovers user attitudes, whereas behavioral research sheds light on user behavior. You will probably find yourself doing both kinds of research at your library, employing both methods but for different purposes. Sometimes you need to gauge member satisfaction with something (say a new service or resource), and other times you want to know more about how members actually *use* something (a new interface or service desk, for example). No one type of user research is better than another, but some techniques are better at uncovering user attitudes, opinions, and behaviors than others. That's why it's important to choose the technique that works best for what you're trying to get out of the research.

This is also a good time to point out our own bias when it comes to user research. As a discipline, UX design tends to place more value on behavioral research than it does on attitudinal research. That's because UX design is all about designing our interfaces, tools, services, and spaces in a way that's mindful of the way our users actually *use* all those things, not so much how they *say* they use them or what their opinions are of them. That is not to say that we discourage the use of attitudinal research methods, nor that we advocate for the use of behavioral methods only; what we are saying is that there are times when you want to get to the heart of your members' opinions about something you're doing (or plan to do), and times when you want to know more about how they use your tools to accomplish their goals. A good user research program employs both types of methodologies to provide a well-rounded understanding of your members so that your decisions are as well-informed as they can be.

Attitudinal Research Methods

SURVEYS There probably isn't much we can say about surveys that you don't already know. Libraries know surveys—we've done them for years, we share survey instruments, and some library sectors even have standardized survey tools that they use to collect longitudinal data and compare results across institutions over time. The one thing we will stress here is that a survey is an attitudinal methodology, which means that surveys are great for collecting data on user attitudes and opinions but not so good for finding out about user behavior. So it's best to use surveys accordingly—ask questions about attitudes and opinions, not about behavior. There are much better ways to learn about user behavior. More on that soon.

Chapter 4: Service Points
Checkpoint 4.3: Members receive assistance when and where they need it

FOCUS GROUPS A focus group is a handful of library members brought together to participate in a guided discussion on a specific topic. As an attitudinal research methodology, focus groups are a good way to engage your members in a discussion, inform yourself of their needs and goals with respect to the library, and gather feedback on their opinions. To get the most out of your focus group, make sure that the group is small (no more than eight participants plus a facilitator) and that the topic is specific (for example, ask about a specific service or resource), and target your questions so that you uncover attitudes and opinions. Common pitfalls to watch out for with focus groups include groupthink and one person dominating the conversation. Aim for unique opinions and inclusion.

Chapter 8: Using the Library

Checkpoint 8.2: Collections are relevant to member needs

USER INTERVIEWS As the name suggests, a user interview is quite simply a one-on-one interview with a user in a conversational format, with questions and prompts to guide the conversation. As a methodology, user interviews straddle the line between attitudinal and behavioral research, making it one of our favorite user research methods. From a good user interview, you can gather a large amount of information on both user opinions as well as behavior, and thanks to its open-ended, conversational nature, you can steer the interview as needed and gain clarification along the way.

Chapter 8: Using the Library

Checkpoint 8.5: Library services and programs solve problems

Behavioral Research Methods

CONTEXTUAL INQUIRY Contextual inquiry boils down to watching people in their own environments or contexts. The very best way to understand your members is to simply observe how they behave, which is what makes contextual inquiry such a valuable research methodology. While it's tempting to assume that we all engage in contextual inquiry every moment of every day (as long as we have our eyes and maybe our ears open), the truth is that contextual inquiry isn't as simple as watching how one of your members interacts with a self-check machine as you walk by on your coffee break (that's more of an anecdotal observation). Contextual inquiry actually requires dedicated attention and focused time during which you observe multiple subjects in their pursuit to accomplish a specific task. Contextual inquiry requires a surrendering of assumptions, keen observation, rapid note taking, and time to synthesize the data and reflect on what actions to take, if any.

Chapter 3: Physical Space

Checkpoint 3.4: The building supports diverse behaviors

JOURNEY MAPPING Journey maps describe the paths people take to accomplish tasks when using a particular service. These maps are often graphical displays of various touchpoints and the actions that connect them. For instance, a library might map out the process of picking up an item from the reserve shelf. Or, better yet, you might ask one or more of your members to map out this process for you, making this a useful behavioral research method.

Let's stick with the reserve pick-up example. The touchpoints and actions to complete that task might include the following:

- Place hold on library website
- Receive notification email
- Travel to library
- Park in lot
- Enter building
- Walk to reserve shelf
- Locate item
- Walk to circulation desk
- Interact with library worker
- Exit building

Once you actually list and map out these steps, it becomes a lot easier to identify the specific touchpoints that cause friction. And once you know which touchpoints cause friction, you can aim to rework just those. The end result is an improved overall experience as a result of improving select touchpoints.

Chapter 6: Signage and Wayfinding

Checkpoint 6.8: First-time visitors can easily locate all parts of the library

USABILITY TESTING Usability testing is closely related to contextual inquiry because most usability tests involve observing a user attempt to accomplish a specific task or series of tasks. Where usability testing diverges from contextual inquiry is in the guided nature of most usability tests, wherein the test facilitator interacts with the user to ask her to carry out the specific tasks that are being observed and tested. Usability testing is most useful for testing interfaces, websites, and other virtual environments to figure out what works and what doesn't, but you can easily perform a usability test in a physical environment as well (for example, you might test the usability of your directional signage by asking members to find specific locations in your library and observing them as they do so).

Chapter 7: Online Presence
Checkpoint 7.2: Members can easily accomplish critical tasks

CULTURAL PROBES Cultural probes are first-person data collection methods for gathering information on test subjects over a period of time. A cultural probe is a simple ethnographic research method in which your test subjects provide the data through vehicles like diaries, photographs, or videos, documenting some specific behavior or activity in which they engage. Cultural probes are useful because they provide a way to collect data over an extended period of time and they shed light on both attitudes and behaviors.

Chapter 5: Policies and Customer Service
Checkpoint 5.7: Service is consistent across the organization

2.2 Other User Research Techniques

There are a few other techniques we discuss in this book that don't fall into either the attitudinal or behavioral categories of user research and a couple that aren't user research techniques at all. They are, however, all useful techniques you can employ to ensure a more user-centered approach to the way you design your interfaces, services, and spaces. We'd like to round out this discussion with a brief overview of each.

Card Sorts

A card sort is a participatory design methodology that uses a series of cards and labels to determine user preferences for how to organize something. Most often, card sorts are used in the web development process when developers are designing site navigation and making decisions about navigation labels. In that specific instance, you might do a card sort with a handful of your members to help you determine how to structure your site's architecture and navigation and how to label your top-level navigation items. Card sorts are not just useful for informing web development work; you can perform a card sort exercise with your members any time you want their input on how to organize or label something—for example, when you need to organize a physical collection or label your directional signs.

Chapter 7: Online Presence
Checkpoint 7.5: Content is written for the web

Personas

Personas are fictional depictions of an organization's audience. As we've already noted, knowing your audience is key to developing services and resources that are useful and meaningful to them, which is why we are such big proponents of user research. But even with a well-developed user research program at your library, it's sometimes easy to forget who your members really are and what their goals are. This is where personas come in. They provide a surefire way to ensure that everything you do is designed in the most user-centered way possible. Once you've done enough user research to know who your members are and what they want and need from the library, you can create a series of personas (three to five should do it) to represent different segments of your audience. These composite character sketches will include demographic information (name, age, gender, etc.) as well as some information to capture each persona's behaviors, motivations, needs, and goals.

Chapter 8: Using the Library

Checkpoint 8.3: Marketing materials are relevant to member needs

A/B Testing

As you might have guessed based on the name, A/B testing is a way to test slight design variations with discrete groups of users to track and gauge the success of each design. It sounds complicated, but it's actually a fairly simple design test that is best explained through an example. Imagine a form on your website with two buttons at the end, one labeled "clear form" and the other labeled "submit." If your web team is unsure of what color each of those buttons should be, you have a good candidate for an A/B test on your hands. For the test, you would design two versions of the page (version A and version B), with two different color options for your buttons. You would then randomly serve up a version of the page to your web visitors and track their success in completing and submitting the form. Once you've had the test running for a few days and you've gathered enough data on the use of both versions of the form, you probably have a pretty good idea of which of the two versions works best for your members. A/B testing is particularly useful when you're developing something virtual like a web page, but you can also use it for print marketing materials and when you're prototyping physical space design.

Five-Second Tests

As the name implies, a five-second test is a simple test wherein you show testers a page for five seconds and, once the five seconds have elapsed, ask them to recall what they remember about the page. If you remember playing that party game as a child, where you would have a specific amount of time to memorize as many random objects on a tray as possible, you are already well familiar with five-second tests. For our purposes, the point of a five-second test is to test recall and figure out what elements on a web page stand out the most.

Chapter 7: Online Presence

Checkpoint 7.7: Home page clearly expresses what people can do on your site

Content Audit

Catalogers, rejoice! A content audit is a list of all the content on your website. Yes, every page, PDF, image, and whatever else, all listed in a big spreadsheet. Conducting a content audit helps you take stock of what's on your website and allows you do some useful assessment.

A content audit that lists a page ID, URL, and title is called a quantitative audit. This is useful for seeing the contents of your site and perhaps creating a schedule for keeping pages up to date.

You can go further and create a qualitative audit. A qualitative audit allows you to assess each piece of content on your list according to whether it is useful, usable, current, appropriately written for the web, and more.

Content audits can be a lot of work, especially if your site is spiraling out of control. But considering that the content on your site is the very reason you have a site, content audits are a tool worth using.

Chapter 7: Online Presence

Checkpoint 7.4: Web content is engaging

2.3 Additional Reading

Just Enough Research, by Erica Hall (A Book Apart, 2013), www.amazon.com/
  dp/1937557103

Observing the User Experience: A Practitioner's Guide to User Research, 2nd ed., by
  Elizabeth Goodman, Mike Kuniavsky, and Andrea Moed (Morgan Kaufmann,
  2012), www.amazon.com/dp/0123848695

Interviewing Users: How to Uncover Compelling Insights, by Steve Portigal (Rosenfeld
  Media, 2013), www.amazon.com/dp/B00CEKR872

Studying Students: The Undergraduate Research Project at the University of Rochester,
  by Nancy Fried Foster and Susan Gibbons (ACRL, 2007), www.ala.org/acrl/
  files/publications/booksanddigitalresources/digital/Foster-Gibbons_cmpd.pdf

Adaptive Path's Guide to Experience Mapping (2013), http://mappingexperiences.com

Handbook of Usability Testing: How to Plan, Design, and Conduct Effective Tests, 2nd ed., by Jeffrey Rubin and Dana Chisnell (Wiley 2008), www.amazon.com/dp/B008L03ZOY

Card Sorting: Designing Usable Categories, by Donna Spencer (Rosenfeld Media, 2009), www.amazon.com/dp/B004VFUOL0

The User Is Always Right: A Practical Guide to Creating and Using Personas for the Web, by Steve Mulder and Ziv Yaar (New Riders, 2006), www.amazon.com/dp/B0058NWP9S

The Elements of Content Strategy, by Erin Kissane (A Book Apart, 2011), www.amazon.com/dp/B004ZRFJ4G

Content Strategy for the Web, 2nd ed., by Kristina Halvorson (New Riders, 2012), www.amazon.com/dp/0321808304

Chapter 3

Physical Space

▶ **WAY BACK IN THE INTRODUCTION, WE TALKED A BIT ABOUT THE IMPOR-**
tance of approaching user experience holistically, about how a good user experience
is not just about having a functional and usable website but also about your physical
space—how it looks, feels, smells, sounds, and functions. This chapter delves into
those details and provides some principles to guide you and techniques to explore
in your quest to provide exceptional spaces to your members.

3.1 The Library Building Is Clean and Functions as Intended

Why This Is Important   DIFFICULTY RATING: ★

We hope that it won't take much to convince you that your building should be clean
and functional. It is a basic need in at least two senses: not only is it (hopefully)
a simple checkpoint to cross off the list, but it is also one that should be given
priority. As the physical instance of your library, your building is meaningful and
influences how people perceive the institution.

If you're aiming to create a great user experience but your building is broken
down or dirty, your services will have to be extremely amazing to offset the negative impact of an unpleasant physical environment. Conversely, a well-appointed

and clean building alone can't create great experiences, but it certainly can set the stage.

Assessing Your Library

Here's a checklist for reviewing a library building. You can probably do an objective review, but consider taking this exercise a step further. Ask some library members to help with this. Their fresh eyes will see things that are easy for you to overlook.

As you assess each category, use a simple scale:

0—Poor, needs major improvements
1—Adequate, minor improvements advisable
2—Exemplary, no improvements possible

FURNITURE Furniture should be clean and intact. Make sure there are no stains or holes in the fabric, and no broken parts.

RESTROOMS The fact that this is a sensitive subject highlights how important it is. The state of your restrooms can make or break someone's opinion of your library. Restrooms should be inoffensive, appropriately lit, conveniently located, and always stocked with adequate supplies. The restroom-cleaning schedule will depend on the size of your library and the number of restrooms, but they should be cleaned often. Do library workers use a dedicated staff restroom to avoid using the public ones? That's a bad sign.

WALLS Examine the library's walls as if you're inspecting a newly remodeled room in your house. Does it meet your standards? The following imperfections detract from the overall appearance of the library:

- pinholes
- leftover adhesive from taping up posters
- marks from furniture
- water or other physical damage
- graffiti
- sloppy painting
- dirt around the baseboards

Conduct a room-by-room analysis, and create a document listing necessary repairs.

FLOORING Whether your floors are wood, tile, carpet, or a combination, like the rest of the library, they should be clean. To maintain cleanliness, schedule periodic deep cleanings with your cleaning service or bring in a specialist. If your carpets are beyond cleaning, budget for new carpet or an alternative that will wear better. Floors also need to be safe. Be sure your flooring provides adequate traction in wet conditions and that weather mats don't bunch up and turn into hazards. There are functional and aesthetic concerns with flooring, too. Hard surfaces like tile tend to reflect sound, while carpets mute and soften a room.

Scoring

If your analysis revealed very few 0s and 1s, give yourself 25 points. About half 0s and 1s? You get 12 points. If your building has major problems or scores more than half 0s and 1s, give yourself somewhere between 0 and 12 points. Record your score in the appendix.

Improving Your Score: Cleaning Up

Your assessment can easily be turned into a work plan. Make note of all of the 0s and 1s in a concrete plan for what needs work. Tackle the high-profile areas first (your main entrance and your first floor) and work inward from there.

3.2 The Library Building Is Free from Clutter

DIFFICULTY RATING: ★ ★

Working in the same building every day often results in a certain type of complacency. We become accustomed to our surroundings and—much like what happens with library policy—we accept things the way they are simply because that's the way they are. One thing that is easy to overlook is clutter. Many different things tend to pile up in libraries: bookmarks, brochures, newsletters, computer monitors, unused reference books in a corner (and entire shelves of unused books for that matter), scrap paper and pencils, magazines for sale, computer cords, and flyers on a cork board are examples of the kinds things that can really clutter your physical space. And, often, we're surrounded by such things but we don't even see them. This checkpoint is all about being mindful and adopting a critical eye toward the clutter in your building.

Why This Is Important

SMALL-SCALE CLUTTER We are 100 percent against clutter. Cluttered spaces are unrestful, making them uncomfortable to be in compared to the peaceful experience of being in a pleasant, uncluttered space. Clutter is a symptom of unintentional design decisions: stuff gets shuffled around and added without consideration of how it impacts the bigger picture. We're not saying that your building has to adopt the minimalist aesthetic that we've come to expect from Scandinavian design; all we're saying is that simplicity has a place in every library, no matter the style.

BIG-SCALE CLUTTER Speaking of simplicity, the fewer things in a system, the easier it is to organize and make them look presentable. Take, for an extreme example, a collection of two items; it would be very easy to keep them effectively tidy. Two hundred items? Less so. Two hundred thousand items? Drastically less so.

Again, this isn't just about aesthetics. Ridding your library of clutter makes life easier for your members and has real advantages for staff, too. Consider this example: a library with a display of brochures and bookmarks next to its public computers (you've probably seen such a display; maybe you even have one). This display has twelve items on it, with varying levels of currency and relevance. Hardly anyone takes the time to read all the titles (there are twelve after all), and glancing at them is hit or miss. Our advice for such a display? Cut the number of items in half, then cut that number in half again. Aim for three to four items in the display.

The benefits of having three to four titles are obvious—members can now easily glance at the display and see all titles quickly, allowing them to find something of use to them almost immediately. The maximalists among you might argue that if there are only three or four items, there's less chance that members will find something that they're interested in. Indeed, if such a display is weeded down randomly, that might in fact be the case. But we're trusting the library staff to know what is of interest to members and what is not (let's hope they will do a bit of user research to find that out) and to use that knowledge to trim down the collection thoughtfully. Done right, this exercise will increase the overall relevance of what's left on display while eliminating the options that few if any care about. In this way, reducing clutter not only makes for a more pleasant environment, it increases the usability of the library.

Assessing Your Library

Take the time to open your eyes and really see your library. It might help to do some interdepartmental observations so folks are looking at a different environment with fresh eyes. Take notes. Pictures are a great tool for this exercise because they can powerfully illustrate when there's too much stuff around. Regroup everyone and have a conversation about what you all saw. As we suggested for the first checkpoint in this chapter, about cleanliness, consider having library members help you assess the clutter in your building.

There are at least half a dozen commonly cluttered places in libraries.

COLLECTIONS If you have a solid, and regular, weeding plan for your library, good for you. You already know that library collections are prime candidates for decluttering. If you haven't done much (or any) weeding at your library, now is the time to start. It doesn't have to be an onerous task either: much like how you might look for unused content on your website, you should pore over circulation statistics to find items that aren't working hard enough to justify the space they take up on the shelf. Keeping the classics is one thing, but holding on to *Windows 3.1 for Dummies* is another. Recycle anything that's collected dust.

If it sounds like we're being harsh and cavalier about collections here, it's for a reason. If you work in a massive research library that has a mandate to collect and retain all human knowledge, then you can skip this discussion and move on to the next bit of decluttering advice. But as librarians who have either worked for or with large research libraries, we know that this sweeping collections mandate either no longer exists or is no longer realistic. So if you or someone you work with bristles at the thought of deselecting titles from a collection that has been lovingly built over many years, now is a good time to be reminded that space is at a premium, and if a title isn't getting used, it should seriously be considered as a candidate for removal.

We also encourage you to take a wider view of the collection. Take a look at your reference collection, for example. If your print reference collection isn't already smaller than it was five years ago, now is the time to evaluate it. Maybe most (if not all) of it can be discarded. Another area worth considering is your popular magazine collection. Many titles lose their relevance after a short time, so why hold on to them past their *best before* date? Since magazines can get messy quickly, pulling old ones from your collection will also spruce things up by virtue of having them gone from your shelves.

EQUIPMENT One of the indisputable laws of library service is if you have material in your collection that requires a certain piece of equipment to view/read/access it, then you must also provide access to that equipment. Microfilm is a good example of this—if you have old newspapers that are available only on microfilm, you can't get away from providing access to a microfilm reader so your members can actually read those old newspapers. That's just basic common sense, really. But, as your collections change and you start to get rid of certain formats, don't forget to scale back your equipment offerings accordingly. It will probably come as no surprise to you that libraries often miss this crucial step, holding on to legacy equipment even as their collections in those formats decrease in size and popularity. Those four microfilm machines your library acquired in the 1960s were probably in high demand back then, but how many times have you seen all four in use recently? Maybe it's time to scale back. Same goes for your VCRs, record players, and any other media device that just no longer sees the use it once did.

BUILDING ENTRANCES What if someone came to your house and put free newspapers, public transit schedules, community events flyers, and other advertising in your front entrance? We're guessing you would be horrified at all that excess clutter. We feel the same way about such clutter in library entrances, too, and we bet we're not the only ones. Make sure you're making a good first impression by keeping this area focused and clear of clutter.

BROCHURES, PAMPHLETS, NEWSLETTERS, AND OTHER DISPLAY ITEMS Displays that include brochures and the like often fall prey to the same mechanism of expansion that plagues building entrances: more items keep getting piled on, rendering each one less likely to receive any attention. Be selective in your presentation of these items. Ultimately, aim to be selective in their development, producing fewer, more relevant items in the process.

PROGRAMS AND EVENTS While physical space isn't the problem with superfluous library events, they can clutter a library's mental space. Is your library continuing to host long-standing programs out of inertia rather than enthusiastic attendance? Perhaps it's time to put them out to pasture. Freeing up time and financial resources can enable you to try something new.

SIGNS Putting up a lot of signs can inadvertently create an unrestful environment, especially if they're not well designed. In the future, instead of putting up a sign, try to change the circumstances that are prompting you to do it. Your members will be better served and your space will look better.

Scoring

You can score up to 20 points on this checkpoint. Use your best judgment to assign an accurate score. Is your library filled to the brim? Perhaps you'll receive only 10 or fewer. Is your library the paragon of order and calmness? Give yourself 15 or more.

Improving Your Score: Decluttering

There are two steps to decluttering, and both of them can be difficult. First, you need to identify clutter. Next, you need to get permission to clear out that clutter. For something like a display of newspapers, this will likely be easy. Other areas of clutter, like services or programs, are bound to be a bit more sensitive. Since these things are more central to a library's mission, library workers are likely to have strong feelings about them. To overcome potential conflicts, elevate your decluttering discussions from the realm of opinion to user needs. Rely on the methods described in the first two chapters of this book to help you determine what to cut and what to keep.

3.3 Furniture Adequately Supports Member Needs

Why This Is Important   DIFFICULTY RATING: ★ ★

Midcentury furniture designer Charles Eames said that "the role of the designer is that of a very good, thoughtful host, all of whose energy goes into trying to anticipate the needs of his guests." While this hospitable statement applies to all library touchpoints, it is pretty obvious how it specifically applies to the furniture in your building.

The premise of this checkpoint might seem fairly simple. Advocating for comfortable furniture just makes sense because who would conceivably advocate for furniture that's uncomfortable and unusable? Certainly no one who is taking the time to read this book! However, this checkpoint is not just about ensuring that your furniture is comfortable; it's also about ensuring that your furniture is functional in the way it supports member needs as well as your needs.

Take, for example, the conversation we once had with a library director who actually uttered the words, "We don't want the chairs to be *too* comfortable." A passerby might balk at such a sentiment and assume that said library director was harsh and uncaring. However, the rest of the conversation filled in the picture nicely: that director was talking specifically about selecting the right chairs for the library's quick-access computers, which had a five-minute limit on use. In that particular case, the director was simply drawing upon one of the eight principles of UX design that we discussed in chapter 1—he was designing with intent for a specific type of behavior. In other words, if you expect your members to spend no more than five minutes on a specific task, in a specific location, don't put your most comfortable chairs in that location because comfortable chairs will make them want to linger. The environment that you create shapes people's behavior, so do it wisely.

Assessing Your Library

It's easy to determine if your library's furniture is comfortable: use it for a day. Does it feel good? Do you have enough space for your laptop, papers, and coffee mug? Does your back get sore after reading in a lounge chair for thirty minutes? Answering questions like this should be illuminating. But don't stop there. Be sure to ask library members what they think. Prepare a small survey, or interview folks as they're using the furniture.

Determining if your furniture is functional and meeting people's needs can be difficult, but it isn't impossible. As you begin to think about the utility of your library's furniture, it is essential to think about what activities the furniture is intended to facilitate. Here are some common library tasks:

- studying
- reading
- working in a group
- using a laptop
- using a desktop
- attending events
- getting help at a service desk
- finding library items
- checking out library items
- returning library items

Consider conducting some contextual inquiries, observing members as they accomplish these library tasks. Are people wandering around the library looking for a place to set up? Are groups of people working together in spaces designed for individual use? Do members move furniture around to better suit their needs? Are events constantly at capacity?

Here, too, you can ask some questions in person or via a survey. Have members agree or disagree with statements such as "I can always find a space in the library to

use." You can also ask open-ended questions like "The library needs more _____."
However, don't base any major furniture purchases on the answers to these open-ended questions. Remember, people's opinions and their behaviors are often two different things. Look for high-frequency responses and use them to confirm or rethink your hunches.

Scoring

After observing or conducting a survey, or both, assign yourself up to 20 points. If you provide comfortable spaces for all types of library users adequate to their needs, you get full points. If your furniture is severely lacking or inappropriate, you get less than 10. You'll likely fall somewhere in the middle.

Improving Your Score: Improving Comfort and Functionality

The only way to improve uncomfortable furniture is to replace it with comfortable furniture. Simple enough, right? Unfortunately, this simple thing gets complicated by the fact that library furniture can be expensive. If you've identified some uncomfortable furniture in your library, rank which pieces get the most use. Replacing these first will have the biggest impact. Chances are you'll have to advocate for some funds to complete this project. As always, ground this conversation in user needs. Use the data you've collected to help make your case, and be sure to include some photographs of contorted people sitting in awkward positions.

When it comes to improving the functionality of your furniture, there's not a whole lot we can say without knowing your particular requirements, needs, and constraints. But here are three things that we can advise:

- Take your cues from your members. If they are constantly rearranging furniture on a regular basis, observe what they do and try to make changes accordingly.
- If your problems require you to buy some different furniture, buy furniture that can be easily reconfigured for different purposes and evolving needs. Think of how your library might change in the next five years and make sure your new furniture will be able to adapt.
- As we mentioned earlier, be intentional in the furniture decisions you make for your library. Different types of furniture provide different cues, so take those cues into account when buying pieces and arranging them in specific locations. The next checkpoint delves into this a bit more, so keep reading.

3.4 The Building Supports Diverse Behaviors

Why This Is Important   DIFFICULTY RATING: ★ ★

A lot of different people use libraries for a lot of different reasons. For instance, one person might want a calm space to use her laptop, while others might need a space to collaborate on a group project. Each of these activities is legitimate and each requires a different environment. How can we ensure that all our members are comfortable and able to successfully complete their activities, especially when some of those activities are incompatible with each other? We can create different zones to support different behaviors.

Zoning your library is a cooperative approach to managing behavior. Not only do attempts to enforce unreasonably strict behavior guidelines create an adversarial relationship between the library and library members, they're also not very effective. Clearly, there are much more productive ways for library staff to spend their time than being the noise police.

Assessing and Scoring

If your library staff receives a lot of complaints about specific behaviors, like noise or food consumption, this is a really good indication that different members' needs are in conflict with each other. To really assess how you're doing, spend some time observing members in your building. For example, you might look for competing activities happening in the same location—like members trying to work in groups and individually.

Pick a two-week period to conduct your contextual inquiry. At the end of the two weeks, score 20 points if your members' activities proceed harmoniously most of the time, 15 points if you observe some conflict, and 0 points if you observe a lot of conflict.

Improving Your Score: Supporting Diverse Behaviors

If your library scored poorly on this checkpoint, we recommend setting up zones for different types of activities. While this might sound like an expensive prospect, it doesn't have to be. In fact, sometimes zoning happens organically since different departments are usually in different parts of a library building. You might not even realize it, but many libraries (maybe even yours) already have experience creating zones for different behaviors: many of us have a space dedicated to the sometimes boisterous social learning that goes on during a storytime program or hands-on workshop; some libraries have reading rooms where even the clicking of keyboards is verboten, let alone talking. Draw on this experience to make sure your members can accomplish their varied tasks.

Something else to keep in mind here is how both the types and setup of your furniture can have an impact on how well your zones work. In the previous checkpoint, we discussed the importance of having furniture that supports member needs. In this checkpoint, you need to add consideration for how your furniture selection and setup impact your intentions. For example, if you want to zone a particular area to be conducive to quiet, individual work, you probably want to select individual study carrels and desk chairs; if you want to zone an area for group work, you should probably opt for large tables and chairs; and if you want to zone an area for casual socializing, couches and coffee tables will communicate that message. Of course, there are countless options other than the ones we've just outlined, but the point is that the type of furniture you select for an area can communicate what sort of activity should happen in that area, so it's important to be intentional in the furniture decisions you make for each different zone.

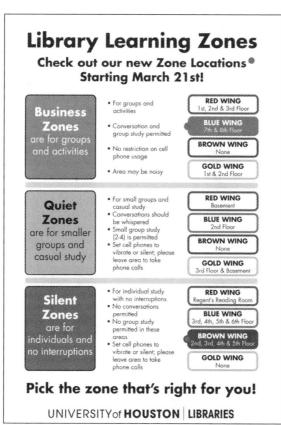

fig. 3.1
Building-zone signage from the University of Houston Libraries.

Once you've delineated zones in your building, make sure you're using more than your furniture choices to let people know what those zones are and what behavior is allowed in each. We like the approach taken by the University of Houston Libraries because it expresses a clear message and features easy-to-read typography (see fig. 3.4).

If your library is small, it might be trickier to implement zones because noise from one area can carry throughout a very small building. One option for creating a zoning-type situation is to plan for different behaviors during different times of the day or week. If your library is very small, you're probably already doing this by default. Storytime hour is expected to be a bit hectic—after school, too—whereas evenings might be a bit quieter. Instead of creating zones based on space, consider creating zones based on times.

3.5 Members Have Easy Access to Power Outlets

Why This Is Important   DIFFICULTY RATING: ★

If you've ever searched all over an airport or meeting room for a power outlet only to find one already occupied or annoyingly out of reach, then we don't need to tell you why this is important. It's frustrating, right? Save your members this frustration by making sure everyone who wants to is able to plug in a device. Or two.

Assessing Power Outlet Needs

We can't provide any hard and fast guidelines for how many power outlets you need because, quite obviously, everyone's needs will differ—depending on the size of your library, the size of your community, your building capacity, your electrical infrastructure, and all sorts of other local issues that are unique to your library. So instead of giving you a firm number, we give you advice on how to determine that number for yourself.

Spend some time observing people using your library. Put a few people on the job, and be sure to pay attention to the number of people using outlets at different times of the day during different times of the year. This is a great opportunity to survey members about an issue, too. But instead of writing and releasing a formal survey, just talk with some folks you see using electronics in the library. Ask them how often they use devices in the library and if they've ever had trouble finding power. They will probably give you a good idea of whether you're providing enough outlets or if you need to add some more.

Scoring

If you're successfully powering up your members, give yourself 15 points. If people are waiting their turn for some juice, 0 points. We think the average library scores about 7 points.

Improving Your Score: Providing More Power

Since most libraries were built before the ubiquity of digital devices, they weren't built to accommodate people using and charging their laptops, e-book readers, phones, and tablets. Maybe your building is already meeting members' power needs, but if you observe members or library staff resorting to drastic strategies to find power, or if you've received feedback requesting more outlets, consider these strategies.

ADD MORE If your building doesn't have many outlets, you might simply have to get some more installed. This will take the services of a professional electrician, true, but depending on the wiring in your building, it might not be prohibitively expensive. Get some quotes to see if it is feasible. A very flexible solution we've seen in a couple of libraries is a grid of power outlets on the ceiling supplying pull-down extensions on retractable cords. Such extensions could be used to power a row of computers or power strips. The added bonus of this arrangement is that the library's furniture is completely configurable without having to take power points into account since they can be made available almost anywhere.

NEW FURNITURE If your current infrastructure will support it, you can buy tables and chairs that provide easy access to power outlets. While this is an expensive option, it is also extremely user-friendly.

POWER STRIPS Creating more power points could be as simple as a few strategically placed power strips. For an added bonus, use something like E-filliate's Power Strip Liberators, short extension cords that allow people with bulky power packs to use the power strip.

DEVICE-CHARGING STATIONS Sometimes people just need somewhere to charge their devices while doing something else in the building. We've seen handy device-charging stations at airports that make use of a small surface with many outlets in a row where people can charge a number of devices. And if leaving devices unattended is a problem, we've also seen device-charging lockers, where members can slide their device into a locked compartment, grab the key, and go.

If you add extra power outlets, you run the risk of adding a mess of cables to the mix, so make sure the solution doesn't create an aesthetic problem. There are a variety of inexpensive products to help with this:

- CableBox: this shoebox-sized device, from the design firm Bluelounge, hides power strips, power packs, and more.
- Cable covers: covering extension cords can help you route them more effectively and create a more professional appearance.
- Hook and loop cable ties: these are handy for bundling unwieldy cords.

Chapter 4

Service Points

▶ **IN OUR ORIGINAL PLAN FOR THIS BOOK, WE CONSIDERED INCLUDING A** chapter on reference services and another chapter to cover circulation services. However, as we started writing those chapters, we quickly came to the realization that dividing content along those lines was perpetuating an occupational bias— libraries tend to be organized that way because those distinctions reflect different specializations in our profession. It's really not a *user-centered* way to think about service points and service desks, and it certainly doesn't reflect the way *users* approach service points in our buildings.

Ultimately, we decided to combine the checkpoints about physical service touch-points into this one chapter because we firmly believe that if we want our organizations to be truly user-centered, we need to get away from planning them around our traditional silos and instead design them the way our members use them.

So in this chapter you will find checkpoints that relate to all types of service desks. Most libraries have at least one service desk and, for many of us, our service desks tend to be hubs of activity in our buildings, so we think they're pretty important. As you will see, the checkpoints in this chapter mostly rate high on the difficulty scale, and that's because changes to service desks aren't easily undertaken, whether those changes are physical or philosophical. We've organized the chapter so that the slightly easier ones come first and the really complex ones follow.

4.1 **Members Readily Approach Service Desks**

DIFFICULTY RATING: ★ ★

What do your service desks look like? Are your members comfortable approaching them to get help, or are they tentative and apologetic about asking for help at your desks? In this checkpoint, we discuss the issue of the physical proportions of your service desks and provide some ideas for how to make them more approachable and comfortable for your members.

Why This Is Important

Once you've had a chance to read the chapter about policies and customer service (chapter 5) and complete the exercises recommended in that chapter, then you'll discover what it means to craft a service philosophy for your organization. Take a look at that service philosophy and reflect on the experience you are trying to provide to your members through that philosophy. We bet there's some focus on things like friendliness, engagement, and approachability. Now look at the physical service desks in your library. Do those physical structures convey the same philosophy? Do they read the same way? Do your desks look friendly, engaging, and approachable? If so, well done! You can move on to the next checkpoint (and maybe even the next chapter!). If not, keep reading.

The days of the large, imposing service desk, staffed by the stern, authoritative librarian, are effectively over. If your library is still living with such a relic, we'd happily point you to all those articles in the library literature that discuss how likely it is for library members to approach such desks (the short answer: not very likely at all). The fact is, large, imposing desks are intimidating to most users. If you've ever tried to provide service from one, you know that it doesn't matter how much you smile and make eye contact with tentatively approaching members. Chances are, they'll still apologize before asking their questions, because the massive, imposing desk you're sitting behind doesn't read as a friendly, approachable structure. It's time to change that.

Assessing and Scoring

So often, the design of physical objects is totally subjective. You might look at the service desk in your children's area and think it's the funnest, most whimsical and approachable service desk you've ever seen. But when you put a four-year-old in front of it, he runs away crying because he's terrified by it. So the best way to assess the approachability of your service desk is to ask the people who matter most in this scenario, the people who you *want* to like and use your service desk: your members.

To assess how your members feel about your service desk, we recommend a couple of exercises. The first is an exercise borrowed from the realm of participatory design. Set up a whiteboard beside your service desk, and at the top of the board, write the following question: "Do you think this physical desk looks approachable and friendly?" Draw two columns beneath the question, one labeled "yes" and the other "no." Leave a marker with the board and encourage members to vote by placing a checkmark in one of the two columns. Score 10 points if more members voted "yes" than "no." Save your score and add it to the results of the next exercise.

Since the first exercise draws purely on the opinions of your members, this second exercise is behavioral and therefore intended to provide some balance in your research results. For this exercise, ask staff to keep a tally of the total number of interactions at the service desk for a week and to make note of every interaction that begins with an apology. (You've heard them before; they usually go something like this: "I'm sorry to bother you, but can I ask you a question?" or "I'm not sure if I'm in the right place, but I have a question.") If you get more questions that begin without an apology than ones that do, score 15 points. If you get more questions that begin with an apology than ones that don't, 0 points for you. Add your score to the one from the previous exercise and record it in the appendix. (There's a 25-point maximum for this checkpoint.)

Improving Your Score: Becoming More Approachable

If your library scored poorly on the two exercises above, you're going to want to make some changes to your service desk. Here are a few ideas for how to accomplish that, listed from easiest to most difficult.

GET OUT FROM BEHIND THE MONOLITH We've been talking about roving information and references services in libraries for decades. One easy way to eliminate the imposition of a massive service desk without the expense of dismantling it and carting it away is to just step out from behind the desk and provide service from in front of it. We bet your members will stop even noticing that monolithic desk behind you if all they see is an approachable, smiling staff member in front of it.

REMOVE BARRIERS Take a look at your service desk. Are there counters or risers or other barriers between the staff members that work the desk and your members? If so, remove those barriers. Take down counters and remove risers. Often service desks were designed with those additions to hide unruly hardware wiring, but nowadays, there are better solutions available to minimize and hide the wires coming out of your service desk computers (wireless peripherals, cord management systems, etc.).

DOWNSIZE If you can remove a surface or two to reduce the size of your service desk, we recommend doing just that. As we mentioned previously, large, monolithic desks are often intimidating just because of their sheer size. Scaling back that size will do wonders.

START OVER If you are in the fortunate position of having money in your budget to do a massive renovation, then we recommend tearing your desk down and rebuilding it entirely. Many of the principles we discuss in this book will help, as will any research you do into service design. You would also be well served to do some fieldwork on your own. Visit other service establishments (read: not libraries) to see how they design their service desks. We can learn a lot about service design from government offices, banks, and triage desks at hospitals, for example. And don't overlook retail. One of our favorite service desk designs (and service models in general) can be found at your local Apple Store. Apple's Genius Bar concept lends itself fairly well to library services and could work quite nicely in your library.

4.2 Service Desks Adjust to Changing Needs

DIFFICULTY RATING: ★ ★

Do you have a favorite spot to hang out in your house? We all do. We're guessing that your favorite spot changes depending on the time of day, or the weather, or the season, or what you're doing at any given moment—working on your laptop or reading a book, for example. Sometimes, your favorite spot might just be too cold, or not sunny enough, or too distracting for what you're trying to accomplish. So you pick yourself up and find another spot that is more conducive to what you're doing. How great would it be if we could do the same thing with our service desks?

Why This Is Important

There are many reasons why having the ability to adjust our service desks just makes sense. If, for example, you have an information or reference desk at your library, you probably deal with everything from quick directional questions to in-depth reference questions at that desk. Standing-height desks are fine for quick informational exchanges but not ideally suited to in-depth consultations. And if you've ever assisted someone in a wheelchair from a standing-height desk, you know that if you could only adjust the height of the work surface, the interaction would be much more comfortable for both you and the person you're helping.

If you've done any furniture shopping for your library in recent years, or even if you've browsed longingly through a commercial furniture catalog, wishing you had the funds to buy new furniture for your library, you've probably already seen all the lovely and varied furniture available for commercial uses nowadays. A lot of this furniture is modular and easy to assemble, so you can snap additions on and off and make changes easily as your needs change. Much of this furniture is also movable, with built-in functionality and conduits to accommodate things like lighting and wiring, making your service desk truly reconfigurable and even mobile. So if you don't like the way the sunlight is hitting your eyes this afternoon, you can pick up your desk and move it (maybe even wheel it) to a better spot a few feet away.

Assessing and Scoring

Assessing the adjustability of your service desks should be a snap: either they are adjustable or they aren't. However, depending on the service desk situation at your library, you might find that there are degrees of adjustability and that your desks may or may not be able to adjust *to the degree* that you would like them to. So, to really assess this, we recommend doing an assessment of everything that is wrong with your service desks. Ask staff who work those desks to list every issue they have with the desk, and once you have that list, figure out how much of it can be changed without any effort (i.e., minimal time and no cost to make the adjustments). If more than half the issues can be fixed with little effort, score 25 points. If less than half the issues can be fixed with little effort, score 12 points. If none of the required adjustments can be done without some effort or cost, 0 points for you.

Improving Your Score: Increasing Service Desk Flexibility

If your library scored low on the assessment for this checkpoint, you might just have to bite the bullet, get rid of your current desk, and get something new. The ideas we present in this section can help you select your new desk. If you scored in the middle range and you actually do have some flexibility to adjust your service desk on the fly, these principles can provide some guidance on adjustments to aim for.

SERVICE DESK DESIGN INVOLVES STAFF It's a good idea to involve desk staff in the design of the service desk from the outset and to keep them involved throughout the entire process—from the conceptual phase, well past the installation phase, to the point where you're assessing how well the desk works a few weeks after living with it. The chances of ending up with a service desk that is not functional/adaptable to staff needs are minimized when you involve staff in the design process from the get-go.

SERVICE DESKS ARE NOT BOLTED TO THE FLOOR It should come as no surprise that the single easiest thing you can do to increase the flexibility of your service desk is to not bolt it to the floor. Even if you're not aiming for a service desk that you can move on a daily basis, not bolting your desk to the floor will give you the flexibility to make changes when you need to at less or no cost.

SERVICE DESKS ADJUST TO THE ERGONOMIC NEEDS OF STAFF AND MEMBERS There are ergonomics professionals who can do an assessment of your service desk. If you work at an academic library, you might even have such professionals on staff and on campus. And even if you don't, your library's health and safety committee can probably direct you to such a service. It's a great idea to get an assessment done so that your service desk works optimally for both staff *and* members. A professional assessment will tell you exactly how flexible your desks need to be to accommodate different ergonomic needs. One standard to aim for is a height-adjustable desk (and chair)—not only to allow your staff to stand or sit at the desk but also to allow them to adjust the height of the desk to optimize the comfort of your members as well (especially useful for anyone in a wheelchair, for example).

SERVICE DESKS ARE MODULAR Modularity is a bit of a buzzword in the commercial furniture word at the moment. Really, all modularity does is allow you to reconfigure your service desks any way you want or need to. Most modular service desks consist of a series of parts that you can add or remove depending on your situation, whether those parts are work surfaces, drawers, shelves, privacy panes, or whatever else you might want to customize and reconfigure. While you probably won't need to make modifications like this on an ongoing basis, in the long run, modularity is more cost-effective because it means you can buy additions or choose to remove parts of the desk as your needs or services change. The opposite of modularity is the custom-built service desk that can't be modified at all—definitely a costly choice we all should be moving away from.

SERVICE DESKS ALLOW YOU TO RECONFIGURE YOUR SPACE WITH MINIMAL EFFORT We've heard of libraries that have turned their entire first floor into giant lecture halls or movie theaters. We've heard of libraries that have had local media move in to cover important local events. We've heard of libraries that have been used as relief areas during natural disasters or other crises. We've heard of libraries that have turned their atriums into cocktail reception spaces for city council events. We've heard of all these unforeseen (and often unplanned for) uses of library spaces, and we can't help but think, if all those libraries had monolithic, unmovable service desks in these open areas, none of those unforeseen events could have taken place at those libraries. All of which is to say that it's a good idea to design/buy/build service desks that you can roll away with minimal effort if/when you need to.

4.3 Members Receive Assistance When and Where They Need It

DIFFICULTY RATING: ★ ★ ★

A few years ago, there was a great commercial on television for a hardware store. A lonely, bewildered shopper walked the cavernous aisles of the store's competitor, desperately seeking out an employee to provide some guidance. Eventually, the shopper spotted an employee at the end of a very long aisle, and in a moment of profound relief, called out a pleading "Excuse me!" to which the employee turned around, looked sheepishly at the shopper, and ran in the other direction. The obvious point of the commercial was for the store to proclaim how much easier it is to find help at their stores compared with their competitors. Ever since that commercial aired, one can't help but imagine employees scurrying away as soon as you enter *any* store!

The good news is, for all the libraries we've worked in and with, we've never encountered a staff member taking off in the other direction upon being approached. The bad news is, we *have* encountered that fundamental problem that befalls anyone in the service sector: providing help to our members when and where they need it.

Why This Is Important

Here's a pop quiz for you: What's the opposite of "when and where they need it"? If you answered "when and where we provide it," you would be correct. The next question is, Which of the two is user-centered and which is library-centered? Yes, that's a rhetorical question; no, we're not going to answer that.

Even though you might consider your library to be user-centered, you may still be designing your services in a way that's more convenient for you than for your members. A classic example of this, one that we have seen in action more times than we'd care to admit, is the library that decides to offer a new service (say IM reference), but only for a few hours, and only in the middle of the day, because that's the easiest time to find staff to operate the new service, not because that's when members need or would use it.

On the one hand, we're ready to congratulate such libraries for taking a step in the right direction—knowing their members well enough to know that this new service is something they need. On the other hand, it's obvious they haven't gone quite far enough in that direction—knowing what your members need is important, but offering a service in a way that is not useful to those members is almost meaningless.

While this argument is most easily illustrated by looking at an example of a new service, we encourage you to think about your existing services in the same way. Even the oldest, most standard library services could probably stand to be looked at and reassessed with a fresh lens. Take your circulation desk, for example. For starters, if you're still referring members to your "*circulation* desk"—a prime example of library-centered language—you may already be losing the battle. (Try "loans," "borrowing," or "checkout" instead.) Think also about the number of service desks in your library. Do you have more than one? If you do, is that because different departments in your organization provide the different services available at those desks, or is it because that's what makes sense and works best for your members? We have a pretty good idea of how most libraries would respond to that question, but you should answer it honestly for your own library.

Assessing and Scoring

The best way to assess how your library is doing on this checkpoint is to implement a simple exit survey. Since providing help when and where your members need it is important in both physical and virtual environments, it's a good idea to administer this survey both in person and online. Both modes can use a variation on these two simple questions:

1. Did you need help finding what you came in for today? (Yes/No)
2. If yes, did you have trouble finding the right person to help when you needed it? (Yes/No)

Score 25 points if your members answer "no" more than "yes" to question 2, 12 points if the responses are evenly split, and 0 points if they choose "yes" more than "no" on question 2.

Improving Your Score: Less "Us," More "Them"

If your library scored less than perfectly on the assessment for this checkpoint, we've got a few ideas for you to consider to boost your performance when it comes to providing truly user-centered help.

ASSESS Before making any changes to your service offerings in the interest of being more user-centered, it's a good idea to do a bit of assessment first. Use the results of your exit survey as a jumping-off point to take a good, hard look at your service offerings. How were the in-person results compared to your virtual results? Are your physical members doing better than your virtual members, or vice versa? Use that data to help you decide where to focus your attention first. Once you've made that decision, why not invest some time and effort in doing some user research? Employ an attitudinal method like user interviews to really get to the heart of your members' needs and goals. If you have time, try a cultural probe exercise, too, to get a better sense of how your library and services fit into members' lives. We can't stress enough that understanding the needs of your community first is the single most important step you can take in developing services for your members, when and where they need them.

COMBINE One of the biggest points of confusion we've witnessed in various libraries (public, academic, you name it) is "desk confusion," a.k.a. not knowing which desk to approach for which purpose. Part of the reason why question two of the exit survey in this section asks about the availability of the "right person" (rather than just *any* person) is that while members may have no trouble finding someone to help them when they need it, they might not always find the *right* someone. One good way to eliminate desk confusion is to combine your service desks into a single service point and cross-train staff to the extent that any staff member can handle ninety-five percent of member needs. Even if you decide that combining service desks would do a disservice to your members, consider cross-training staff anyway. If your members can accomplish ninety-five percent of their goals at *any* service desk in the library, we bet they will be pretty happy.

ELIMINATE It would be shortsighted for us to not mention the radical idea of eliminating your service desks altogether. Depending on your context (budget, administration, staffing, appetite for massive change, community, etc.), you may not work at a library that would even consider this, and that's okay (for now . . . maybe). But if you do work in a forward-thinking and innovative institution with an administration and staff that are willing to consider a radical shift in how you provide service, now might be the time to consider getting rid of your service desks altogether. We all know informational and reference services can easily be handled by roving staff members (as long as they are readily identifiable by your members), and even if you don't have self-check machines in your library for self-service checkouts, staff can be furnished with wireless, handheld barcode scanners to check out materials to members anywhere in the building. We think it's worth exploring the possibility that maybe the best solution to desk confusion is no desk at all.

4.4 Members Receive the Kind of Assistance They Need

DIFFICULTY RATING: ★ ★

Have you ever spent time at a company's website desperately hunting for a telephone number you can call to talk to a customer service rep? You browse through the "contact us" and "about" pages, your disbelief growing exponentially with every click, as you discover that either this organization has decided to eliminate telephone service entirely or made the decision to bury the telephone option as best it can, so that customers will resort to the other modes the company has decided to support more, like online help videos or live chat service. If this experience is not foreign to you, then you know all about that special kind of frustration you feel when you can't interact with an organization using the mechanism or modality that works best for you.

Why This Is Important

Perhaps unsurprisingly, the scenario outlined above describes the actual customer service situation at one very large, multinational telecommunications company (which shall remain nameless). When analyzing that particular scenario, it doesn't take a whole lot of critical examination to figure out that that telecom company is clearly putting its own needs (cutting costs, making more profit) above that of its customers (the ability to contact customer service in a modality of their choice). When libraries make similar decisions that result in benefiting the organization to the detriment of member needs, those decisions tend to seem less egregious because libraries are not motivated by profit. But if those decisions result in a poor experience for members, we think they're just as bad.

What might such a decision look like in a library? Here's an example we see all the time: items like staplers or pairs of scissors chained down to furniture! We know you've seen them too, maybe you even have some in your library. Why do we chain down the stapler? Because if it isn't chained down, someone might walk away with it. A library staff member might recognize that the chain poses a slight inconvenience to members, but we might nonetheless see it as a necessity. To a member? That chain is not just inconvenient, it's also unfriendly and maybe even downright offensive. So, we ask, is the price of a replacement stapler really worth inconveniencing and maybe even offending your members? We think not.

In the last checkpoint, we focused on the importance of providing members with help when and where they need it; this checkpoint completes that equation by highlighting the importance of providing members with the *kind* of help they need. That could be anything from providing help in all the modalities that your members desire (in person, online, over the phone, etc.) to covering the spectrum from self-service to full support to providing one-on-one or one-on-few help, as needed.

Assessing and Scoring

The thing about this checkpoint is that while there might be a baseline against which we can all measure ourselves, *your* library's success in this arena really depends on what *your* members need and how well you're meeting those needs. As such, every institution will vary, so we recommend using an attitudinal research method to gauge how well your members think you're meeting their needs at the moment. As you did in the last checkpoint, you might try implementing a simple exit survey that asks the following questions:

1. Did you need help finding what you came in for today? (Yes/No)
2. If yes, were you able to get the kind of help you wanted? (Yes/No)

Score 25 points if your members answer "yes" more than "no" to question 2, 12 points if the responses are evenly split, and 0 points if they choose "no" more than "yes" on question 2.

Improving Your Score: Providing the Right Kind of Assistance

If your library scored poorly on this checkpoint, you have some work to do in supporting your members' goals and providing the kind of assistance they might need. In the following list, you will find a few ideas that could be useful to any library, as well some ideas that will help you learn more about your members in particular so you can develop services with them in mind.

SELF-SERVICE TO FULL SERVICE There's no single perfect level of service that works for everyone. Some like to troubleshoot and figure things out on their own; others like to watch a quick video before trying something on their own; still others work best with an expert at their side, walking them through every step. You probably have members at both ends of the spectrum and at every point in between, so it's a good idea to define the spectrum of services at your library and make sure you've got a range of services that works for most. So if you're thinking of the spectrum of options in reference help, for example, you would include online guides, self-paced tutorials or videos, searchable knowledge bases, and staff-mediated help.

COVER ALL MODALITIES   Remember the telecom customer service scenario at the start of this checkpoint? Don't be that telecom! Provide service in as many different modalities as you can afford—in person, email, telephone, and real-time chat.

FLEXIBLE IN-PERSON SERVICE   Sometimes the one-on-one model of drop-by, in-person help doesn't fit every situation. In academic libraries, for example, your students might benefit from being able to book an appointment with a librarian at a time that works for them. Or a group working on the same project might want to get some time with a librarian. In both situations, the drop-by reference desk set-up isn't conducive to the kind of help these students need, so you would do well to allow for flexibility in taking appointments and working with groups at a time and place that works for everyone.

FACILITATE CONNECTIONS   If you have the means, you might consider a mechanism that can connect your members to each other for help. Your community is probably full of experts in their own fields, so why not help them find each other? Social media might be able to help here, as can an expertise database for your community, hosted and maintained by the library.

DIVE DEEP   As we've already noted, a library's success in this checkpoint is directly related to how well that library meets the needs of its community of members. To get a really good sense of how you're doing, and to take steps to do better, you'd be well placed to dive deep and do some user research. Here are a few things you might want to try:

- Scenario development with your members. This is a participatory design technique where you work with your members to develop a number of scenarios in which they might need help from the library. Once you've developed the scenarios, you can then brainstorm together for ways the library might provide the kind of help needed.

- User interviews. Talk to a handful of members (five to seven should do it) about the situations in which they seek assistance in their daily lives. Don't bring the library into it—just talk about general help-seeking scenarios and activities and when/how help is sought in each instance. This should give you some insight into the ways your members generally like to get help. Use this insight when planning your service offerings.

- Develop personas. Take a look at chapter 2, section 2.2, for a brief introduction to what personas are and why they might be useful for your library. If you develop a set of five personas that represent your library's users, you can use those personas to assist you in developing the kinds of services those personas need and will use.

4.5 Additional Reading

"LUV and War at 30,000 Feet," by S. C. Gwynne, *TexasMonthly*, March 2012, www .texasmonthly.com/story/luv-and-war-30000-feet

> This article details how customer service and a positive organizational culture have been central to the success of Southwest Airlines.

Service Design Tools, http://servicedesigntools.com

> This collection of resources can help with service design projects at your library.

Setting the Table, by Danny Meyer (New York: HarperCollins, 2006), www.amazon .com/dp/0060742755

> A favorite of a library with excellent customer service, the Darien (CT) Library, this book contains wisdom from successful restaurateur Danny Meyer.

Chapter 5

Policies and Customer Service

▶ **POLICIES AND CUSTOMER SERVICE ARE DIFFERENT, BUT RELATED, EXPRES-**sions of the way an organization feels about people. Maybe we're taking a bit of a leap by assuming some standard heuristics here, but we think there are a handful of universal principles of good customer service for which all libraries should strive. These principles have become our checkpoints for this chapter.

Use these checkpoints to assess the state of the policies and customer service at your library.

5.1 Your Library Has a Service Philosophy

DIFFICULTY RATING: ★ ★

Here's a quick and fun test you can perform: at the next retail store you walk into, ask the first staff member you see what the store's service philosophy is. Chances are, if it's a big retail chain, it probably does have a service philosophy (a quick Google search will give you your answer), but can its frontline staff members tell you exactly what that philosophy is when asked? Do the same thing for any retail or service establishment you visit and for the next few customer service phone calls you get. Keep track of your results. Conclude your mini field experiment by asking the same question at one of the service desks at your library. If the staff member you ask responds by rattling off your service philosophy perfectly, and with a smile, then congrats! You can skip this checkpoint (and the next) and move right on.

We're guessing that most of you are still here. And that's okay. Because we've got a lot to say about service philosophies, what they're good for, why you need them, and how you can come up with one for your library.

Why This Is Important

When questioned about why they do what they do in their workplace, many people answer with a simple "because it's my job." Practically speaking, there's nothing wrong with that; we do what we do because that's our job, and most of us need a job to survive. All that aside, we believe that, especially when it comes to working with the public, service gets better when it is guided by a set of principles that everyone knows, believes in, and practices. One way to think about those principles is as a service philosophy.

Assessing and Scoring

Does your library have a service philosophy? If so, 5 points for you. Add an extra 5 points if you actually *call* it a service philosophy.

Improving Your Score: Creating a Service Philosophy

Quite simply, a service philosophy is a statement or series of statements that outlines the organization's approach to service. Depending on the organization, it might also be called the corporate philosophy or customer service philosophy, or some variation on that theme. A service philosophy is a document that is intended to both guide staff in their interactions with customers and inform customers of what they can expect from the organization in terms of service.

A quick Google search will give you countless examples of service philosophies, but here are a few that we like.

Zappos Family Core Value #1: Deliver WOW Through Service

WOW is such a short, simple word, but it really encompasses a lot of things. To WOW, you must differentiate yourself, which means doing something a little unconventional and innovative. You must do something that's above and beyond what's expected. And whatever you do must have an emotional impact on the receiver. We are not an average company, our service is not average, and we don't want our people to be average. We expect every employee to deliver WOW. (http://about.zappos .com/our-unique-culture/zappos-core-values/deliver-wow-through-service)

Cambridge Libraries and Galleries

Personalized service: Serving people with care. Our patrons are all individuals, and we want to treat them as such. We will strive to provide personal one-on-one service with courtesy, warmth and wisdom. (www.cambridgelibraries.ca/about)

The Ritz-Carlton Credo

The Ritz-Carlton Hotel is a place where the genuine care and comfort of our guests is our highest mission. We pledge to provide the finest personal service and facilities for our guests who will always enjoy a warm, relaxed, yet refined ambience. The Ritz-Carlton experience enlivens the senses, instills well-being, and fulfills even the unexpressed wishes and needs of our guests. (http://corporate.ritzcarlton.com/en/About/GoldStandards.htm)

Crafting a Service Philosophy for Your Library

A good service philosophy is one that resonates with both staff and your members. Here are a few things to keep in mind when crafting a service philosophy for your library.

KEEP IT SHORT No one wants to read a service statement that is pages long. Not staff, and certainly not your members. Your service philosophy will have a lot more impact if it's short and pithy.

MAKE IT USER-FOCUSED, NOT LIBRARY-FOCUSED You can craft all sorts of procedures documents that show staff how to put your service commitment into practice. Your service philosophy statement is not the place for that. Instead, focus on making a statement that your members will understand and appreciate, your promise to them for what they can expect from your library.

INVOLVE STAFF IN THE PROCESS OF CRAFTING THE PHILOSOPHY There are entire books devoted to how to create a corporate mission and values in a way that resonates with staff and gets their buy-in from the get-go. This isn't one of those books, obviously. A simple bit of advice we can offer here is to encourage you to include staff in the service philosophy design process. Here's how:

1. Create a small team that includes staff members from every level. Go heavy on the frontline staff and light on management (one member of management is more than enough).

2. As a group, begin by digging into what's already out there (no need to reinvent the wheel). Research service philosophies from organizations in all industries. Get every member of the group to present three of their favorites, with reasons why they're favorites.

3. Again as a group, decide on three favorite service philosophies from the batch. Break down each to figure out what it is in each that resonates with the group.

4. Create your own service philosophy statement using all the principles you liked from the others.

Throughout the process, communicate often with all staff by keeping them abreast of the group's activities and sharing results from every step. Once you've completed step 4, share the draft of the team's philosophy with all staff to get their feedback. Revise and finalize your service philosophy statement accordingly.

5.2 Your Staff Members Know and Live Your Service Philosophy

DIFFICULTY RATING: ★ ★

Congratulations, your library now has a service philosophy! That's an important early step on the road to really becoming a user-centered organization. And if you went through the process to come up with a service philosophy as outlined in the last checkpoint, you've probably already got the buy-in of most of your staff, which is key to how you will score on this checkpoint.

Why This Is Important

You already know how crucially important it is to have a service philosophy. However, as important as it is, we're here to tell you that just having that service philosophy isn't enough: you also need to live it. In fact, having and publicizing your service philosophy and *not* living it is worse than not having one at all! Making promises to your community and not following through is detrimental because it adds an element of untrustworthiness, undermines your credibility, and could have a long-lasting impact on your library's reputation in your community. Which is the exact opposite of what any library wants. So we rank this checkpoint as even more important than the last.

Assessing and Scoring

Testing your library on this checkpoint requires a two-pronged approach. First, talk to ten randomly selected library staff members who work in public service positions. For each person who can tell you what the library's service philosophy is, award yourself 1 point (10 points max on this element!).

Once you've determined how staff members perform in remembering your service philosophy, you're going to want to test how much they actually live it. This one is trickier but not impossible. You've probably heard of the "secret shopper" technique that companies often use to keep tabs on their employees—to test their product knowledge, upselling techniques, customer service commitment, and all manner of other things. While we are loath to encourage libraries to spy on their employees, we do think it's reasonable to set expectations for what employees should know and do and to test those expectations from time to time. When you're trying to determine your staff members' commitment to your service philosophy, employing a secret shopper is a great way to get to the heart of it.

Of course, there are many ways to use the secret shopper model to test your staff's uptake of your service philosophy. You can do it unofficially by simply asking your friends and family about their experience interacting with staff at the library. You could enlist a family member to approach specific service points and tell you about how he was treated. Or you could actually hire a secret shopper to undertake a set number of specific interactions with service desk staff and score them on how much those interactions live up to the library's service philosophy. You know your organization best, so we believe you are the best person to decide which of these methods would work best for you. To score this element, perform five secret shopper exchanges (however you see fit) and award 1 point for each interaction that proves that the staff member has actually taken the service philosophy to heart and lives it every day. There's a 5-point max for this element and a 15-point max for this checkpoint in total.

Improving Your Score: Ways to Encourage Your Staff to Know and Live Your Service Philosophy

It's easy enough to be excited about something when it's fresh and new. You might find that in the early days of crafting and launching your service philosophy, staff are excited about it and take it to heart. As an organization, the tough part is keeping them excited about it. Here are some ideas to help you accomplish just that.

REPEAT, REPEAT, REPEAT Never underestimate the power of simple repetition. When you say something repeatedly, it tends to stick. Tap into this rudimentary psychology by reminding staff of your service philosophy at every opportunity you can. Print poster-sized versions of the statement and hang them all over your library (especially in places where staff will see them). Print index card–sized versions (if you heeded our advice and kept it short, this should be easy!) to hand to new employees. Or if you have a new employee handbook or training manual, print your philosophy statement on the first page. Always make sure that when you remind your staff about your philosophy, you do so in context, because you don't want to start sounding like a broken record. So, for example, every time you make a decision or change something in the library, preface your notification to staff with something like, "In keeping with our philosophy of X, we've decided to X." Replace the Xs as appropriate.

MODEL GOOD BEHAVIOR Good behavior can be infectious! Nothing spells a commitment to a service philosophy like seeing other staff members model that philosophy and behavior. If you don't work in a service position yourself, treat your customers (who might well be staff members) in the same way you expect them to treat your members.

PROVIDE INCENTIVES We freely admit that the notion of enticing staff with rewards just to get them to treat people well is troubling at best and disingenuous at worst. So instead of creating an employee recognition program to reward your staff for living your service philosophy, you might consider ways to encourage staff to reward each other, or members to award staff, for providing good service. This sort of peer-to-peer (or customer-to-staff) recognition is less patronizing than the usual top-down employee recognition program and is usually better received by employees as well, being a more authentic form of recognition.

REVEAL THE SECRET SHOPPER If you're going to test staff on their uptake of your service philosophy, you should tell them so. Revealing your secret shopper (whether you employ an actual secret shopper or use one of the more informal approaches outlined above) will encourage staff trust and send the message that you're serious about the implementation of your service philosophy.

HIRE APPROPRIATELY We've been known to say that skills are easier to train for than attitude. We wholeheartedly believe that libraries are service organizations and that not everyone can work in a service position. So alter your hiring practices to recruit people with attitudes that best fit your culture and service philosophy.

REVIEW AND REVISE Nothing keeps your service philosophy fresh like a routine review and revision. Make it a priority for your organization to review your service philosophy once every eighteen to twenty-four months. If you engage all staff in the review process, you are essentially taking the pulse of the organization (and staff) by asking yourselves if this is still something you believe in and can continue to embrace. Revise your statement accordingly.

5.3 There Is as Little Policy as Possible

DIFFICULTY RATING: ★ ★

At first glance, the idea of having few policies might seem counterintuitive. Policies provide the basis upon which we build our services, so you might expect that having a policy to cover every possible interaction or scenario just makes things clearer for staff members and manages your members' expectations appropriately. We tend to take a slightly different approach to policies, as outlined in this checkpoint.

Why This Is Important

The way we prefer to approach the issue of policies is to think of them as unnecessary restrictions. Too many policies can limit your staff members in negative ways—they can restrict their ability to exercise their best judgment in how they interact with, respond to, and provide service to members.

One of the best examples we've seen of this notion is the customer service policy at Nordstrom. They have a famous "One Rule" policy for how employees should interact with customers. That rule is, simply, "Use good judgment in all situations." Nordstrom is legendary for having an employee handbook that consists of no more than a single index-size card that lists their "one rule" and makes a point of reiterating that there are no other rules. (See http://about.nordstrom.com/careers and *The Nordstrom Way to Customer Service Excellence*, by Robert Spector and Patrick McCarthy.)

So how can fewer policies improve the user experience at your library? A couple of ways. For starters, it helps minimize staff confusion. The rationale here is simple: the fewer policies you have, the easier they are to remember. If your organization is laden with a policy for every possible scenario, chances are your frontline staff will have to pull out and consult a hefty manual during every interaction with a member. That's just cumbersome and unnecessary. Additionally, fewer policies empower staff to use their best judgment and really put the member first (more on this in the next checkpoint).

Assessing and Scoring

It would be tempting (and easy) to just ask you to count up all your current service-related policies and subtract a point for every policy you have. Instead, we propose a slightly more reflective exercise to assess the state of the policies at your library. Try this: keep a "No List" at every service desk at your library. Get staff at each desk to write down every question or request from a member that results in a "no" response from a staff member. Keep your "No List" for at least a month; then at the end of the month, comb through all the scenarios and list every policy or practice you have in place that necessitated a "no." Starting with 15 points, subtract a point for each policy on that list. Record your score in the appendix. If you've got more than fifteen different policies on your list, 0 points for you!

Improving Your Score: Take a Good, Hard Look at Your Policies

If you scored poorly on the assessment for this checkpoint, your library might be suffering from policy bloat. We have a few ideas for how to fix that.

REVIEW ALL YOUR POLICIES Ask tough questions about each of your policies, including why it was established in the first place and if you really need it anymore. It's alarming how many policies persist for the simple reason that "we've always done it this way."

ENLIST THE HELP OF FRONTLINE STAFF Your frontline staff members are probably the ones who deal with your policies most regularly and therefore know them the best. Get them involved in the policy review by asking them to list the three most useless, cumbersome, or difficult-to-enforce policies they have to work with. Get rid of the useless, retool the cumbersome, and rethink those that are difficult to enforce.

REVISIT THE "NO LIST" REGULARLY It's a good idea to redo the "No List" exercise on a regular basis, say once every two years or so. This exercise can go a long way in evolving your organization from a culture of "no" to a culture of "why?"

5.4 Library Policies Empower Staff

DIFFICULTY RATING: ★ ★ ★

We've already talked about how too many policies can contribute to a less than excellent user experience while at the same time make your staff feel bogged down and encumbered. In this checkpoint, we explore the fact that it's not just the *quantity* of policies that can be problematic. The *quality* of those policies is also worth taking a closer look at. Even if your library is not suffering from policy bloat and you scored a full 15 points on the last checkpoint (congratulations!), this checkpoint is equally important to your pursuit of a superlative experience for your library's members.

Why This Is Important

Sometimes a lot of rules, guidelines, instructions, and policies are just what we need to get our jobs done. If you work at a cutting-edge web startup and the only policy you were told to follow was "throw out the manual and do the best you can," you might feel liberated by that policy. But if you made a living assembling IKEA furniture (yes, such people do exist; I know, I've employed one), you would be very poorly served if that were your only guideline. Why? Because it takes a whole lot of other rules and instructions to succeed at assembling IKEA furniture!

Luckily for us library people, there isn't a lot of IKEA furniture assembly being done in our organizations, at least not by our frontline staff, and not at the request of our members (although what an innovative service opportunity that would be!). So we are in the fortunate position of being able to slough off all those extra policies and craft just a few concise ones that work to empower our staff members to operate nimbly and use their best judgment to make decisions on the fly.

We've already extolled the virtues of Nordstrom's One Rule when it comes to customer service: "Use good judgment in all situations." Obviously, the idea here is to empower your employees to use their best judgment. To do that, you have to trust in their decision-making abilities. And if you trust in their decision-making abilities, you empower them to use their best judgment. See how that works? It's a self-perpetuating win-win situation.

Assessing and Scoring

This one is not quite as easy to assess as some of our other checkpoints. In this case, what you really want to do is figure out whether the policies you have in place at your library empower your staff or, instead, hinder their ability to provide great service. To score how your library fares here, we suggest another two-pronged effort. First, survey ten randomly selected frontline staff members to find out how they felt when they last had to enforce a library policy. Did it make them feel encumbered in their ability to provide good service? Or, instead, did they feel empowered to provide good service? Score 1 point for every time a staff member said enforcing a library policy made him feel empowered.

For the second type of assessment, we recommend drawing on one of the attitudinal research methods we outlined in chapter 1, to see how your members feel about the type of service they've received. For example, you could do a very quick survey of ten randomly selected members. As they leave a service point in the library, ask them if they felt that the service they just received was tailored to their particular need and situation. In this instance, it's probably a good idea to preface the question by asking about the purpose of their visit to the desk because the question about the service they received might not be pertinent in all situations. Here again, score 1 point for every time a member said the service she received was, indeed, personalized to her particular need.

There's a 20-point max on this particular checkpoint.

Improving Your Score: Ways to Empower Your Staff through Policies

If your library scored poorly on this checkpoint, don't be disillusioned! Using policies as a way to empower staff rather than prescribe specific behaviors is a break with what many organizations have done in the past, so we all probably have some work to do. The following are a few strategies that we think will help.

HEED THE LAST FEW CHECKPOINTS We hate to bang the same drum over and over, but we will when we have to. The truth is, we honestly believe that having a service philosophy, living that philosophy, and paring back the number of policies at your library are three vital steps that will get you started down the road to empowering your staff to provide the best service they can.

CHANGE YOUR CULTURE We don't suggest this one lightly. We know you're not going to change the culture of your organization overnight, which is one reason why this checkpoint is rated as a three—this one is going to take a lot of work. You will need the buy-in of senior administration, as well as buy-in from your governing body, whether that means the library board (if you're a public library) or getting the blessing of your dean/university librarian/director/provost (if you're an academic library). In this context, changing your culture is about two things: making service (and, therefore, the user experience) your number-one priority and investing in your staff accordingly.

HIRE THE RIGHT PEOPLE Yet another idea that's not going to happen overnight. We mentioned not too long ago that we are big proponents of hiring for the right attitude rather than for specific skills. Probably every HR executive will tell you that skills can be taught, but attitude can't. Some people were born to work in service positions and others simply weren't, so aim for the former when you're filling front-line positions. Seeking candidates who have worked in retail or the service industry is a good place to start.

CRAFT ONE LAST POLICY The irony of telling you to craft a policy to empower your staff is not lost on us. But the policy we have in mind here is specifically about empowerment, so hear us out. One of our favorite employee empowerment tales comes via the Ritz-Carlton, the luxury hotel chain. In the first checkpoint in this chapter ("Your library has a service policy"), we quoted the Ritz-Carlton's credo as an example of one of our favorite service philosophies. To back up that credo, the Ritz-Carlton has a whole philosophical and cultural scaffolding in place to support their staff in living that credo—including a motto, three steps of service, clearly defined service values, and "the 6th Diamond," a proprietary statement about exemplary service (for all the details, see http://corporate.ritzcarlton.com/en/About/GoldStandards.htm). In addition to all that, each staff member in the organization is entrusted with $2,000 to spend on each guest at the staff member's own discretion. In an article in *Forbes* magazine in 2009, Simon F. Cooper, then-president of the Ritz-Carlton, had this to say about this level of commitment to service:

> When you say up to $2,000, suddenly somebody says, wow, this isn't just about rebating a movie because your room was late, this is a really meaningful amount. It doesn't get used much, but it displays a deep trust in our staff's judgment. . . . The concept is to do something, to create an absolutely wonderful stay for a guest. Significantly, there is no assumption that it's because there is a problem. It could be that someone finds out it's a guest's birthday, and the next thing you know there's champagne and cake in the room. A lot of the stuff that crosses my desk is not that they overcame a problem but that they used their $2,000 to create an outstanding experience. (www.forbes.com/2009/10/30/simon-cooper-ritz-leadership-ceo network-hotels.html)

So this policy at the Ritz-Carlton effectively empowers its employees by showing a high level of trust in their ability to make good decisions for the benefit of their customers. While we don't mean to suggest that you rush out and create a policy that empowers each employee at your library to spend thousands of dollars on each member, we do think that it's worth thinking about what tools you *can* put in your employees' hands to empower them to create amazing experiences for your members. Perhaps the ability to forgive up to a certain dollar amount in fines per member? Or enabling them to use their discretion in the enforcement of particular policies? Whatever you decide will work best at your institution, craft a brief policy around it and make sure your staff members know about it and live it. If your organization has made a commitment to service and you've hired the right people, this one is a no-brainer.

5.5 Staff Members Are Friendly and Genuinely Want to Help

DIFFICULTY RATING: ★ ★ ★

We've repeatedly made the point that good customer service is a vital part of a good user experience. We sincerely believe that human interactions can make or break a situation. Ever had a delicious meal at a restaurant ruined by an unfriendly server? Ever had a delay-ridden flight be redeemed by a flight attendant who went the extra mile to make sure you were comfortable? Both are prime examples of how an interaction with a person can equally ruin a good experience or redeem a bad one. This checkpoint is all about the centrality of good customer service to the experience of your members at your library.

Why This Is Important

You've probably heard the old adage about how when someone has a good customer service experience, they might tell one or two people, but when they have a bad experience, they tell ten times that many people. That alone should make you realize how important it is to sit up and pay attention to the state of customer service at your library. The other thing that should get your attention is something else we've said repeatedly in this chapter—that skills can be taught but a good attitude can't. That statement is never truer than when applied to customer service. That is, good customer service can't be taught or faked; good customer service requires smart hiring.

This checkpoint receives a "difficult" rating for a couple of reasons. Firstly, if your organization hasn't always valued good service highly, then you might be dealing with frontline staff members who aren't quite up to muster when it comes to customer service skills. Secondly, even if you are in a position to hire new frontline staff, it isn't necessarily easy to find people with a gift for customer service.

Assessing and Scoring

To assess how well your organization does on this checkpoint, we recommend going straight to the best judges of the customer service experience at your library: your members. Use an attitudinal research method like a survey to ask fifteen of your members if the service they received on their last visit was friendly and if the staff members they interacted with seemed genuinely interested in helping them (note: we've suggested a lot of surveys in this chapter; you might want to roll them all into a single customer service survey, so as not to subject your members to survey fatigue). Try to make responding to the survey as anonymous as possible—you can hand out fifteen surveys in person, but encourage respondents to drop off completed surveys to another location like a box on a service desk. Studies have shown that people often won't complain in person if they receive less than adequate service, so you might find members telling you the service they received was fine when their written comments show otherwise. Score 1 point for every member who had a positive experience for a 15-point maximum.

Improving Your Score: Improving Customer Service

We fully acknowledge that most of these ideas aren't ones that can be implemented overnight, which is another reason why this checkpoint is rated "difficult"—the sorts of changes we're suggesting here will require administrative approval, some extensive discussion and negotiation with any labor groups representing staff members, and staff buy-in in general. Making a commitment to service is easy, whereas living that commitment takes time and effort, as these ideas illustrate. But we hope you will agree that the goal of improving the customer service at your library is worth it.

EMPOWERMENT REVISITED The last checkpoint was all about empowering your staff members to use their own discretion to create amazing experiences for users. If you have the right frontline staff in place, implementing this should be fairly straightforward, not to mention fun. If you don't have the right staff members in place (yet), you might want to come back to this later.

REPOSITION STAFF As we mentioned above, if your organization is only just beginning to make service a priority, you might be saddled with frontline staff members who lack that certain finesse when it comes to interpersonal skills. If you find yourself in this situation, you might consider a reorganization to transition these staff members to backroom duties that get them out of direct contact with library members but at the same time harness their skills effectively. If a person is not cheerful and friendly on the front lines, chances are he isn't comfortable in such a position anyway, so moving him away from the front lines might well be doing him a favor. At the same time, trawl your staff complement for people who *are* people-focused, but who might be doing backroom work, and reposition those people to service positions.

HIRE THE RIGHT PEOPLE You saw this recommendation in the last checkpoint, and we think it's important enough to repeat it here. If you are in a position to hire frontline staff (lucky you!), make sure you hire people who are not only genuinely friendly and helpful but also have empathy. Look for people with experience working in retail or the service sector. An experienced mentor once said that she likes to hire people who have worked as restaurant servers into frontline positions at her library. The rationale? Restaurant servers work well under pressure, can multitask, and are usually well versed in good customer service habits.

ENCOURAGE TRANSPARENCY Nothing shows a commitment to customer service like encouraging feedback from your community on how you're doing and being transparent about it. Set up a comment board in your library and online to encourage your members to tell you how you're doing. (For the online equivalent, employ a social tool like Facebook or Twitter, or consider a customer service platform like Get Satisfaction, http://getsatisfaction.com.) Be real and authentic in how you respond to those comments, too—accept praise graciously and apologize when you need to.

BUILD EMPATHY We've made it a point to say (many times) that a good attitude can't be taught. However, we do think that *empathy* can be taught, or at least surfaced and honed. A great way to encourage your staff to take ownership of the service experience at your library is to make them understand what the experience of using the library is really like for your members. And the best way to build that understanding and, therefore, empathy, is to make them walk a mile in your members' shoes. To do that, institute a "Work Like a Patron Day" for your frontline staff, an idea first championed by librarian Brian Herzog (www.swissarmylibrarian .net/2008/10/07/work-like-a-patron-day). On that day (which we'd probably call "Work Like a Member Day," to use our preferred term), your staff should try to carry out as many of their daily tasks as possible using the same tools, resources, and interfaces that your members do. As Herzog recommends in his blog post, staff should

- enter and leave the library through the public entrance (not the staff doors)
- use the public restrooms
- use the public computers to work
- reserve public meeting rooms for meetings
- follow all library policies

You might also consider having staff use the same furniture that members use, and encourage them to use public interfaces (as opposed to staff interfaces) for all your online tools. Encourage staff to write down their observations, be reflective about the experience, and take some time on the following day to debrief as a group.

Another, similar, way to build staff empathy is to conduct a contextual inquiry exercise with frontline staff. As we briefly discussed in chapter one, contextual inquiry is a behavioral research method wherein participants observe members trying to accomplish specific tasks in the library. A successful contextual inquiry exercise with your staff will require some training ahead of time, when staff are encouraged to surrender their assumptions, observe keenly, take notes, and have lots of time at the end of the exercise to synthesize the data they've collected and reflect upon what they've observed. Once again, debrief as a group to give staff members a chance to discuss what they observed as well as the exercise in general.

We think you will find that exercises like Work Like a Member Day together with contextual inquiry will build the empathy of your staff members and transform them into better service ambassadors for your library.

5.6 Service Is Consistent across Departments and Modalities

DIFFICULTY RATING: ★ ★ ★

We're both firm believers in the idea that libraries are *all about service*. We're convinced that everything we do is a service, whether that's holding a storytime event for five-year-olds, helping someone print their resume, ordering an article for a member via interlibrary loan, or designing an interface to browse the library's new resources online. Granted, all these services are probably done by different groups of staff in different departments and through different modalities (some in person, some online, some over the telephone). But we're here to remind you that, as far as your members are concerned, they're all services, and they don't really care which department provides which—they just want some consistency in the way they're provided.

Why This Is Important

If you've paid any attention to Twitter recently, you've probably witnessed (or maybe even experienced firsthand) an instance of service inconsistency across modalities. Whereas Twitter made its start as a moderate corner of the web, where friends could hold brief conversations with members of their network, it is now an enormous customer service platform, where every corporation worth its salt has a presence that is probably being monitored by staff that was hired just to respond to tweets about the company (complaints, plaudits, you name it). For customers who are on Twitter, this is great! They get quicker, better, more candid service there, so they're thrilled. For folks who aren't? Too bad for them, they have to continue to deal with annoying phone trees and long wait times at customer service call centers.

The point is, we don't think it's okay to offer better service to some customers just because they opted to use the newest, most cutting-edge platform. Just like we don't think it's okay to offer better service to a library member who is standing in front of us at a service desk, compared to the one who chose to email her question to us. *But libraries do this all the time.* We set standards (whether implicitly or explicitly) for services in our buildings, but we don't set the same standards for other modalities like email or virtual reference or social media or telephone service.

Modalities aside, we also think it's important to think about consistency in service across departments. So often, we get stuck in our own silos and end up making decisions about service without stopping to talk to our colleagues in the rest of the building. While it might sound fantastical at a safe distance, we know of more than one library where the cost to photocopy something is different depending on whether a member requests that copy from the interlibrary loan department or the special collections department.

Think this sort of thing doesn't happen at your library? Time to find out.

Assessing and Scoring

Assessing service consistency can be a little tricky. First of all, it's important to compare apples to apples, so you might start by making a list of similar services that are performed by more than one department or in different modalities by the same department. Take reference service, for example. You might provide reference service in person, via chat, and via telephone, and you might have more than one department that has a reference desk. If so, that would be a good candidate for comparison and assessment. You could compare policies/practices on lineups and wait times across all your reference service modalities and desks. Or there's our photocopying example. If you have more than one department that provides copying services to members, that would be another good candidate for comparison and assessment. Or take a look at the programming that happens at your library. Does more than one department offer drop-in or sign-up programs or events? If so, it might be worth taking a closer look at how each department handles sign-ups or waiting lists, for example.

To score your library on service consistency, we recommend comparing three different services with their counterparts in different departments or modalities. You get full marks (10 points) if all three services are consistent with their counterparts, 7 points if two are consistent with their counterparts, 3 points if only one is consistent with its counterparts, and 0 points if there is no evidence of consistency for any of the three services.

Improving Your Score: Increasing Consistency across Departments and Modalities

If your library scored perfectly on the assessment for this checkpoint, we offer our hearty congrats. We've both worked in large organizations, so we sincerely understand how difficult it is to actually reach that level of service consistency. And it's for that same reason that we understand, if you didn't score so well, how service inconsistencies can creep into our practice. Here are a few ideas to help get you back on track to better service consistency at your library.

MAKE THE COMMITMENT Service consistency is one of those things you're going to need administrative support for. Why? Because staff can become entrenched and territorial about the things they do. On the one hand, that's great because it probably means they're taking ownership of their services. On the other hand, they might not be all that willing to compromise and change to better align with other departments (you might hear things like, "We've been doing this for so much longer than they have, why do *we* have to change?"). To balance that entrenchment and territoriality, your library needs to be clear about making a commitment to, first and foremost, improving the user experience. From there, it shouldn't be too much of a stretch to argue that members getting the same type of service from different departments or modalities is just a better experience for them.

TALK TO EACH OTHER Sounds simple, right? And it is. If you encourage your staff to talk to each other more before making decisions about service offerings, we bet you'll see a rapid reduction in service inconsistencies.

ASSESS SIMILARLY If you collect statistics or undertake any sort of assessment of the services you provide at your library, a good step to take in making services more consistent across departments or modalities is to make sure everyone is doing the same sort of assessment or statistics collection. This would lead to evidence-based decisions that would work across departments and modalities, and not in isolation of each other.

EMPLOY THE SAME TOOLS If you have more than one department in your organization that requires members to sign up to attend events, you should all be using the same event registration software. Sounds like a no-brainer, right? It is, mostly. Except, we've seen it happen too many times at various libraries that different departments use different tools or software to accomplish the same thing. That may be fine if those tools are limited to internal or back-end processes, but it's altogether unacceptable if your members need to use those tools.

SET COMMON SERVICE STANDARDS Do you have a standard for wait times in service desk lineups (e.g., members wait no more than three minutes until a staff member interacts with them)? How about standards for turnaround times for email queries (e.g., all email queries will receive a response within twenty-four hours)? If not, those are two (of many) service standards you should be drafting for your library. Most important? Don't draft those standards in isolation—get involvement from all departments in the library. Consistent service standards are crucial in improving general service consistency in any service organization.

THINK HARMONIZATION You might consider undertaking a larger project to harmonize all the services in your library. For this to work, you will need buy-in from all levels, as well as a serious commitment to making changes in the interest of a more seamless user experience. A service harmonization effort should start with a gathering of all the stakeholders in the library who are responsible for offering services to the public. Once that group has been assembled, a good next step would be to begin a discussion of service models for each of the areas represented in the room (get each service area to present all the details of its service to the group) so that everyone is on the same page. Following that, it would be a good idea to inventory all services offered in the library, as well as all the platforms, tools, and resources used to deliver those services (i.e., systems, software, applications, equipment, etc.). Apart from all the consistency and efficiencies you can gain by simply comparing service models and resources, you will also be pleasantly surprised at just how much service harmonization can happen simply by having the right people in the room, talking through common issues.

5.7 Service Is Consistent across the Organization

DIFFICULTY RATING: ★ ★ ★

After that last checkpoint, you might think we've said all we need to say about consistency, but you'd be wrong. While ensuring that service across departments and modalities is crucial, the other kind of consistency we'd like to discuss is equally important to ensuring a high-quality experience for your members. Allow us to explain.

Why This Is Important

Here's a scenario we'd like you to wrap your head around. You're shopping at your local grocery store and you really need to get your hands on some okra because your favorite celebrity chef has just extolled the virtues of gumbo on the morning show. You've asked three different staff members on three different visits to the store if they have any okra. All three staff members apologized and told you that, no, they haven't had any okra for a while and have no idea when they might get some again. And they leave it at that. How does that leave you feeling? Disappointed, surely. Probably a bit annoyed because you now have to visit another store to get your okra fix, and there's no guarantee that you'll find it there, either.

If you had to rate the service you received from your grocery store on all three occasions, you might say it was fine. Consistent, even, since you got the same answer from all three staff members.

Now rewind that scenario to when the first staff member tells you that, no, they don't have any okra, but this time asks, "What recipe are you trying to make? And have you considered substituting eggplant, green beans, or baby green zucchini for the okra because all three of those vegetables are often used as okra substitutes?" And what if the second staff member tells you that, no, they don't have any okra, but to give her a minute to go speak with the produce manager about what's going on with their okra supplier, and when they might expect another shipment? And what if the third staff member tells you that no, they don't have any okra, but asks if you've checked the grocery store three streets over because she's sure she saw some there as she biked past it on her way to work this morning?

Now if you had to rate the service you received from your grocery store on these three occasions, what would you say? You'd probably say it was pretty wonderful.

And was it consistent? Well, not if consistency means getting the same answer every time, from every staff person you spoke to. But if you're asked if the service was consistently above average? You'd probably answer in the affirmative.

Too often, we structure our organizations and policies so that we can achieve that first kind of consistency—the one that ensures that all policies and procedures are clear and that all staff members know those policies and procedures so that they all respond to the same scenarios in the same way. That's both safe in management terms and comfortable in employee terms. In reality though, it's that other kind of consistency, the kind that is all about consistently awesome service, that we should be aiming for. It's way harder to achieve, to be sure, and terribly difficult to train for, but it's worth the effort because it results in an exponentially better experience for your members.

Assessing and Scoring

To assess the service consistency in an organization, you can't do a one-off survey. Consistency is the type of thing that can only really be assessed over time, so we have a couple of suggestions for how you can assess this checkpoint at your library. The first is more involved and will take a bit of planning; the second is a bit easier to carry out. Choose the assessment method that works best for your organization.

OPTION 1: CULTURAL PROBES We discussed cultural probes in the "Behavioral Research Methods" section of chapter 2. For this checkpoint, we recommend recruiting five regular visitors to your library and giving them each a notebook in which to record their experiences after five visits to the library. Tell them to include detailed information on each of their visits, why they were there, who they spoke to, what service they received, and how they felt about that service. Some members might complete their assignment in a week; others might take a bit longer. After each participant has submitted a completed diary, conduct a short user interview with each to gauge the consistency of the service they received. Score 3 points for every participant who says the service was consistently great (maximum 15 points).

OPTION 2: USER INTERVIEWS If you don't have the time to devote to doing a complete cultural probe exercise, you can probably get similar results (although not as rich) by just doing the user interviews described at the end of the cultural probe activity outlined above. Recruit five of your repeat visitors and ask them open-ended questions about each of their last five visits to the library. Make sure you have a note taker with you to write down their responses or, better still, record the interviews if you can so that you can go back to the recordings and reflect on each of their responses (if you are recording interviews, remember to get each interviewee's permission first). Again, score 3 points for every participant who says that the service was consistently great, to a maximum of 15 points.

Improving Your Score: Getting to Consistently Great Service

There are a few ways your score can shake out on this checkpoint. If your user research (the cultural probe exercise or just the user interviews) has told you that you're neither consistent in response (not all staff said the same thing) or level of service (no evidence of great service at all), you'll want to go back to the start of this chapter and work on the exercises we've included in the "Improving Your Score" sections. If you did well in consistency in response (all staff did say the same thing) but scored poorly in level of service, that's okay! You're halfway there; don't stop now. The following ideas will get you over that last hurdle.

LATHER, RINSE, REPEAT This is the final checkpoint in this chapter for a reason— we don't think you can get to consistently awesome service unless you pass all the other checkpoints first. So make sure you've crafted a service philosophy, your staff members know and live that philosophy, you reduce the number of policies you operate under, you empower your staff, and you build staff empathy to make your staff as friendly and helpful as they can be.

ONGOING STAFF ENGAGEMENT If you've introduced the changes we've talked about in this chapter in an effort to improve the service in your library, good for you! But know that you can't just pat yourself on the back now and walk away. This stuff requires ongoing training and reminders. Consider repeating a lot of the exercises we've talked about in this chapter (e.g., secret shopper, the "No List," contextual inquiry, cultural probes) on an ongoing basis. Also make sure that you engage your staff on a regular basis by encouraging them to participate in the ongoing exercises as much as possible and communicating the results of those exercises consistently.

REWARD GOOD BEHAVIOR If you really value good customer service and are committed to it, then you should reward staff members who demonstrate good customer service behaviors. Consider some of the incentives mentioned in the second checkpoint in this chapter.

CONSIDER STAFF ROTATION It's pretty easy to lose your vim and vigor for customer service when you do the same job at the same desk in the same location every day. If you have some flexibility in moving your frontline staff around, consider doing so. Whether that's moving people between branches or just moving them between service points in a particular branch, changing things up once every twelve months can do wonders for keeping staff from becoming bored and losing their empathy. The bonus for the library is a fully cross-trained frontline staff, allowing you to be flexible and nimble toward broader change.

Chapter 6

Signage and Wayfinding

▶ **WHERE AM I? WHAT CAN I DO HERE? WHERE CAN I GO FROM HERE? HOW DO** I find where I want to go?

The signs in your library—ideally—help people answer these questions. They're an important touchpoint, especially for new visitors. These signs not only enhance or detract from the visual experience of your library, but they also affect people's chances of having a pleasant, successful experience.

Think of the signs in your library as a form of customer service and an expression of your library's attitude toward its members. Are they as friendly and helpful as the people in your building? Because signs are tools used to connect people with information, we consider sign design well within the scope of library work.

Use the checkpoints in this chapter to assess and improve the signs in your library.

6.1 Your Library Has a Brand Manual That Is Consistent with the Principles of Graphic Design

Why This Is Important   DIFFICULTY RATING: ★ ★ ★

A brand manual is, essentially, a list of rules for how your signs, print materials, and websites should look. As such, they're inherently prescriptive. Developing this will take some time, yes. Ultimately though, doing so will be a time saver because you won't have to design new signs or web pages from scratch every time you need to create a new one. The design decisions will already have been made, and creating a sign will be as simple as plugging in the right content and applying the style.

This brand manual should be used when creating anything meant for library members: brochures, posters, your website, library cards, signage, tote bags, and everything else. Why is this important? A cohesive style will make your library memorable and recognizable, enabling people to connect with it. It will allow you to consistently express your library's values and personality. It will show that you care about details, which will increase the amount of trust members have in your library. Librarians are information professionals and should treat their information design accordingly. Though it would help, you don't need to be an expert designer to create a brand manual for your library. This checkpoint will help demystify the process.

Assessing and Scoring

Either your library has a brand manual or it doesn't, so this is an easy one to assess and score. Give yourself 25 points if you have a full brand manual, and 0 points if you have nothing. Have something in between? Assign points as you see fit.

Improve Your Score: Creating a Brand Manual

To create this brand manual you will select your library's official typefaces and colors, and provide guidelines for how these things are implemented. Here's a sample table of contents that would create a solid brand manual for your library's style:

Elements
1. Typography—the typeface(s)/font(s) that should be used in all printed materials, from logos and headings to regular text.
2. Colors—the primary and secondary (and so on) colors that should be used on all materials.
3. Logo or wordmark—information about and samples of your library's logo or wordmark.

Templates
4. Signage
5. Posters
6. Brochures
7. Website

Here are some things to consider as you put together your brand manual.

Selecting Typefaces

The foundation of visual communication is letters. These letters can take many sizes and shapes, and choosing the best ones for your library is an important design decision. Selecting typefaces is about more than finding something you think looks pretty. You must also consider a typeface's legibility and ability to communicate your library's values. Choose them carefully because you'll be using them for everything your library produces. Stick with the classics; they're classics for good reason.

Typefaces are divided into two main categories.

SERIFS Serif typefaces have little bits at the ends of the letters' strokes. These bits are called serifs, and they often give typefaces a formal, traditional, and elegant feel.

Bodoni   Garamond
Times   Century

In most cases, serif fonts are good for extended blocks of text meant for long-form reading. Many books are set in a serif typeface (including this one). Popular serif fonts for blocks of text on the web include Georgia and Times.

SANS SERIFS As the name implies, sans serif typefaces lack the ornamental bits at the ends of strokes. Sans serif fonts can give designs a modern, sleek, and friendly appearance.

Helvetica   Frutiger
Futura   Gotham

They are especially effective when used for headlines or signs. Take a look at the signs in any airport, and you're guaranteed to find a sans serif font in use. Note that even though serif fonts are good for long-form reading in print, sans serif fonts are easier to read on many types of screens than serif fonts. Popular typefaces for reading on the screen include Arial and Verdana.

HOW MANY SHOULD I CHOOSE? Probably two. Because the typefaces you select need to work well together, choosing only two keeps things simple and is less complicated than trying to make multiple typefaces work together. A safe bet is to choose one serif and one sans serif. This ensures some contrast between the two.

This example uses a Bodoni header and a Helvetica body:

LIBRARY NEWS
Come to the library on June 6th for face painting.
Kids love this for some reason.

Nice and classic all around. These two fonts are straightforward and legible.

Another good combination would be a Helvetica header and a Century Schoolbook body:

Library News
Come to the library on June 6th for face painting.
Kids love this for some reason.

In these next two examples, notice how the Futura Bold header (right) provides a stronger visual hierarchy and generally works better with the Helvetica body than the Futura Light header (left):

LIBRARY NEWS
Come to the library on June 6th for face painting.
Kids love this for some reason.

LIBRARY NEWS
Come to the library on June 6th for face painting.
Kids love this for some reason.

TOO SIMPLE? Selecting only one typeface can lead to designs that are unrestful, overwhelming, and difficult to parse. If you're going to use only one typeface, consider using Helvetica. If you do this, be sure to increase contrast to ensure your design looks intentional. This example contrasts a Helvetica Bold header with a Helvetica body:

Library News
Come to the library on June 6th for face painting.
Kids love this for some reason.

Developing a Color Palette

There is an infinite number of colors on the spectrum, and choosing the right ones for your library can be daunting. Like the fonts you choose, you should use your selected colors any place you're representing the library. This being the case, when you're choosing colors, make sure you keep in mind that they'll be used for a variety of print materials and digital products, too.

Keep your color palette simple, aiming for perhaps four or five colors (excluding black and white). Including more than that not only makes choosing them more difficult, it also can complicate their implementation.

Before you find some pretty colors, figure out what you want them to express. You'll be communicating with them, so you want to make sure you're sending the right message. Tie this decision into your library's mission and overall attitude. Choose three words and find colors that express these values. Examples include:

- trustworthy, steady, supportive
- fun, current, adventurous
- bleeding edge, humorous, surprising

One great way to match colors to these values is to create a mood board. Hang three pieces of flipchart paper and label them with your values. Put a pile of old magazines, glue sticks and scissors next to them and ask folks to cut out colors and images they think represent each value. Better yet, put this in a public space and have library members do it. It could be really interesting to have both staff and the public do this exercise and compare the similarities and differences.

Once you have a general sense of the colors you'd like to use, you don't have to start with an empty white screen to make your final choices. You can always do a general search for "color palettes" on the web and find some useful websites to get you started. Take a look at COLOURlovers (www.colourlovers.com) and Adobe's Kuler (https://kuler.adobe.com). They'll give you some inspiration and help you choose colors that work together.

Keep track of your color palette by recording each color's hex value (e.g., #8CCCD9) and, if you produce a lot of print material, its Pantone (e.g., Pantone

630—Vintage Blue) and RGB (e.g., 140,204,217) values. The two websites just mentioned can help you determine these.

Designing Your Logo

If you're serious about the overall user experience you're aiming to provide, your library's image, and people's relationship with your library, hire a professional to design a logo (a symbol to represent your library) or wordmark (a type of logo that is a simple text-based representation of your library) for your library. Professionals in training at a local college might be a group to explore as long as you don't commit to using their work.

If you don't have the funds to hire a professional, consider creating a logo or wordmark yourself. A logo to which you've given at least a little thought will be better than one that hasn't been designed with intention. Before you start designing, get some inspiration by looking at some great logos. The work of Saul Bass, Paul Rand, and Chermayeff & Geismar is a great place to start. See the "Additional Reading" section at the end of this chapter for a list of sources to consult.

Next, make a list of some unique attributes of your library and the surrounding community. Are there any outstanding architectural or natural features that could serve as the basis of a logo? Keep in mind that you've already selected some typefaces and colors. Can you use these to produce something effective and appropriate?

Be sure to use a vector-based program such as Adobe Illustrator to create your logo. This will allow you to adapt your logo for many different purposes, including high-quality print formats, and will let you resize it without degrading the quality of the image.

As with all areas of design, keeping things simple will lead to better results generally because there's less opportunity to make mistakes. If you aren't satisfied with anything you've created, opt for a wordmark using one of your selected typefaces.

Plainville Library

Designing Templates

Selecting typefaces and colors is a good start, but there's still more work to do. This next step—creating templates—will guide the implementation of these elements and ensure that the typefaces and colors you selected are used appropriately.

Before you can design templates you have to know what you're designing. If you haven't already done it, now is a good time to conduct an audit of the signs in your library. (See checkpoint 6.2, "All signage uses the same visual language.")

You'll likely find a variety of signs that will each need their own distinct but complementary designs. (See checkpoint 6.3, "Different types of signs are visually distinct.") Once you have a list of the different types of signs in your library, you'll know what sorts of templates to create.

For the sake of this example, we'll create a template for 8.5" x 11" informational signs and illustrate how it can be used.

Layout

Creating grid-based templates will make your life easier and produce a cohesive look for all of your output. Because the resulting columns will dictate where to place text, grids can help structure your designs and make it easier to create a visual hierarchy.

Short on time?

While we recommend creating a template for each type of sign you have in your library, if time constraints prove so limiting that you can't do this, don't give up entirely. Even creating a single, well-designed template for all of the signs in your library will be better than creating none. What's more, with only one template, it won't be as difficult to create consensus and get people to use it.

Before we divide the canvas, we need to create a border because not all of the space on the canvas is usable. Jamming content—especially text—into the edge of your canvas makes things difficult to read and adds tension to the design. Create a border and keep text within it. In this case we'll give the page a ¼" border on all sides (see fig. 6.1).

fig. 6.1
Quarter-inch page border.

To create a grid you'll divide the canvas's usable space. Although there is an infinite number of ways to divide this space, in this case we'll keep it simple and choose five wide columns. This number of columns will be useful without providing so many variables that it adds unnecessary complication. But creating a grid is a little more complicated than just dividing the space into equal parts. Much like we created a border for the canvas, we need to build in some breathing room for the columns. These are called *gutters* (see fig. 6.2). Without gutters, elements on the page can run together and be rendered unreadable.

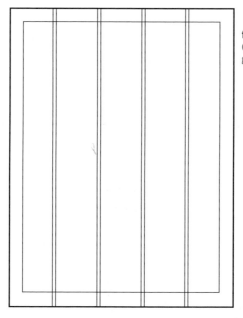

fig. 6.2
Grid and gutters.

Now that we have our final grid, we can experiment with the layout of our informational sign template by arranging elements in different places. But first, what content should we include in our sign? Because this is an informational sign, we'll include the following:

- library logo
- event info
- event date

See figure 6.3 to see what this might look like. Experiment with placing the elements of your sign in different areas of the grid, as in figure 6.4.

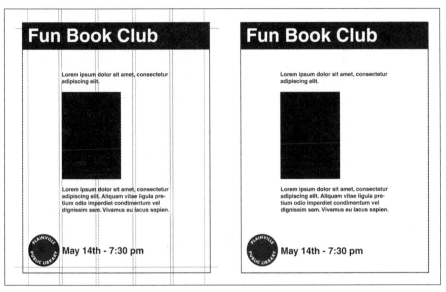

fig. 6.3 Elements on grid.

fig. 6.4
The elements
from figure 6.3,
rearranged.

Creating templates for the different types of signs in your library will make each sign easier to produce and, thanks to their consistent design, easier for members to understand.

A Pattern Library for Your Website

Your website should employ the same typefaces and colors as your other graphic products. Again, just using the same typefaces and colors isn't enough to guarantee a good design. You'll need to guide the layout of your web pages too. An effective way to accomplish this is to create a pattern library. A pattern library is a bit like a template, but instead of, or in addition to, laying out exactly where to put everything on a page, it details how all of the particular elements on a page should look. Even if only one person is designing the site, it will still be a very useful tool. For an outstanding example, see the website demonstration of the BBC's Global Experience Language (www.bbc.co.uk/gel/web/foundations/universal-grid/the-grid). For another excellent example, see Grand Valley State University's UI pattern library (http://gvsulib.com/ui/ and fig. 6.5).

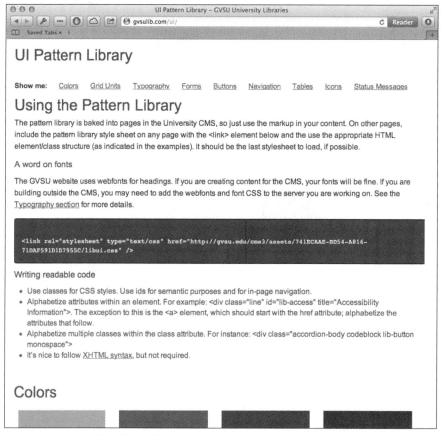

fig. 6.5 Grand Valley State University's UI pattern library.

Create a template for each type of page on your site. Examples of page types include the following:

- home page
- landing or navigation pages
- main section pages
- subpages
- forms

Then detail how things should look on these pages. Developing a pattern library saves time in the long run and is essential for site redesign projects.

Implementing Your New Visual Language

While doing so might be ideal, you may not be able to employ your new visual language to change everything in your library at once. Make a list of every place you'll use this new design—from bookmarks to your website—and create a realistic implementation plan and stick to it. Consistent, measured progress here is good. A halfhearted implementation is ineffective and your effort creating the visual language will go to waste.

Using color effectively

When designing your templates keep these points in mind:

- You'll create a cohesive hierarchy by making sure the same types of signs use the same colors.
- Black is difficult to read when it is over most colors. Stick with black on white only, or maybe yellow. Have you ever noticed that a lot of airports use black on yellow for important signs? Black on yellow is a high-contrast combination that is easiest for most people to read, even at a distance.
- Colored text can be fun, but it can be difficult to read. The safer choice is to forgo colored text and stick with black and white only.
- White text is a safe choice over anything that's dark enough to provide adequate contrast.

6.2 All Signage Uses the Same Visual Language

Why This Is Important   DIFFICULTY RATING: ★ ★

This should be obvious: your library could have the best visual language ever developed, but it won't do any good unless it is implemented properly.

Assessing Your Library

Look at each sign in the library. Does it conform to your established visual language? Take note of those that don't and redesign them. You can keep track of this by conducting a signage audit. The quickest and easiest way to audit all the signs in your library is to take a photograph of each one. Put these photographs in a spreadsheet and list the following:

- Location of sign
- Type of sign (directional, identification, instructional, regulatory, or informational)
- Employs visual language? (yes or no)
- Taped to a surface? (yes or no)
- Appropriately written? (yes or no)

Scoring

Remember, to score the full 15 points here you'll need to have developed a brand manual. If after the audit you've found that all of your signs use the library's visual language as described in the manual, give yourself 15 points. If you found a lot of rogue signs—0 points.

Improving Your Score: Standardizing Signs

Use your signage audit to create a work plan for fixing rogue signs. Don't get rid of your spreadsheet once you're done! Use it for an on ongoing audit, keeping track of any new signs that get created.

Of course, this plan assumes that you've already created a brand manual. If you've already done that, great! Fixing signs will be as simple as making them compliant with the guidelines in your manual. If you haven't developed a manual yet, get to it. Once it is implemented you can revisit this checkpoint and increase your score.

6.3 Different Types of Signs Are Visually Distinct

Why This Is Important   DIFFICULTY RATING: ★ ★ ★

There are different sorts of signs in libraries and they all serve different purposes. For instance, some are meant to help people get from one point to another while others are meant to alert people to a change in policy. When each type of sign has a different visual design, the entire signage system becomes more effective. And while having an effective signage system seems like a fine thing, the end result is what we're concerned with: it will help library members successfully use the library.

Assessing Your Library

Before you can make sure the different types of signs in your library are visually distinct, you'll need to take stock of the types of signs you have. Here are some different types of signs in libraries, adapted from *Interior Design for Libraries* by Carol Brown (American Library Association, 2002):

DIRECTIONAL These signs help library members get from where they are to where they want to be. A common example is a sign with a location and an arrow.

IDENTIFICATION These signs label areas of the library. A typical identification sign (and perhaps a confusing one because of the library-centered lingo) is a "Circulation" sign hanging above the circulation desk. Other common identification signs are those with call number ranges found on the ends of stacks.

INSTRUCTIONAL These signs help people use the library. A common instructional sign is a guide to operating a self-check machine taped next to its screen.

REGULATORY These signs express rules or attempt to influence behavior. Many libraries have signs telling members to not use cell phones in the library.

INFORMATIONAL These signs describe the library or its services. They vary from a library's name on the front of a building to an advertisement of an upcoming program.

As described in the "Assessing Your Library" section of checkpoint 6.2, evaluate all of the signs in your library and record what type of sign it is. Also record whether the sign uses the same design as other signs of its type. If your library doesn't have a formal signage system, chances are that you won't find signs that match.

Scoring

There's a maximum of 10 points for this checkpoint, which you'll earn if all of your signs are in line with each other.

Improving Your Score: Creating Visually Distinct Signs

Remember, each different type of sign should have its own design, but they should all share the same visual language. While creating a visual language for your library isn't easy, the effort you spend will simplify the creation of visually distinct signs. For instance, regulatory and instructional signs could share the same typeface and shape, but be different colors.

Having a uniform scheme can evolve a collection of hodgepodge signs into a complete wayfinding system. Using different colors and shapes is an effective way to do this. For instance, all regulatory signs can be red, white, black, and round. All identification signs can be yellow, black, and rectangular. You'll want to be much more detailed, of course, but all of the specifications should be included in your brand manual.

6.4 There Are as Few Signs as Possible

Why This Is Important   DIFFICULTY RATING: ★

Signs aren't necessarily bad, but they can be symptomatic of a larger problem. Let's look at this issue from a different direction. Ideally, your building wouldn't need any directional signs. It would be so intuitively arranged that spatial and visual cues would inform people about where they need to go. Ideally, your services and equipment would be so easy to use that you wouldn't need to employ instructional signs, either.

As great as it would be to work in such a library, we're not sure one like that exists. All libraries need to use some signs to help people successfully use the library.

However! This doesn't mean that we should put up as many signs as possible. Just like you should remove extraneous content and navigational elements from your website to make the good stuff easier to find, you shouldn't have extra signs around. They're distracting, and they create an unrestful atmosphere. Each sign you erect renders other signs less effective.

Assessing and Scoring

Assessing this is a bit subjective since it is difficult to know which signs are useful and which are getting in the way. Give yourself up to 10 points, depending on how much signage in general there seems to be.

Improving Your Score: Removing Signs

Which signs should you remove? First, we recommend removing any regulatory signs—signs meant to influence behavior—because most of these signs attempt to regulate *exceptional* behavior. In this way, you're forcing everyone to look at something that applies to very few people. Plus, they're mostly ineffective. Is a mere sign telling people that they're not allowed to take drugs in your library's bathroom going to prevent anyone intent on doing that? Handle the occasional behavioral problem politely in person, not with signs.

After you've removed regulatory signs, take stock of the instructional signs in your library. Is there anything you can do to render these unnecessary? This will likely require making substantial changes to something that's been confusing to

fig. 6.6 Doorknob sign.

people. For an obvious example, see figure 6.6.

Removing directional signs at random isn't a smart idea because it's difficult to know which are useful. Instead, we recommending conducting the test described in checkpoint 6.8 ("First-time visitors can easily locate all parts of the library") to learn which directional signs you can get away with removing.

After you've cleaned up your library's visual environment by removing signs, be on the lookout for changes in members' behavior. We doubt you'll suddenly see an increase in rule breaking or inappropriate behavior, and you probably won't find yourself answering a bunch of questions that were previously answered by a sign. If you do, consider the best way to implement an appropriate sign.

6.5 There Are No Paper Signs Taped to Walls, Doors, Tables, Computers, or Any Other Surfaces

Why This Is Important   DIFFICULTY RATING: ★

Taped-up paper signs make us sad. But don't worry about us. Worry about your members. These unprofessional-looking signs have a negative effect on a library's visual environment and detract from members' experiences.

Reflecting upon his involvement with the planning of the central Seattle Public Library, Bruce Mau wrote:

> In the beginning, there was one problem, books, and one solution, shelves. When you go into the library now, there are literally hundreds of signs and pieces of furniture provided to deal with each new format. Everything from magazines to DVDs has a cabinet, a users' manual, an inventory, and an interface. The result is a massive communication problem. While librarians themselves should be commended for their improvisational tactics, overall the patrons confront a constant muddle,

with one organizational layer of information Scotch-taped over another. The time has come to imagine a new way. (Bruce Mau, *Life Style* [Phaidon, 2000], p. 242)

At best, these signs don't look very attractive, and after a few months of getting banged around, they tend to look worn and sloppy. This isn't what we're aiming for, right?

Not only do they look unprofessional, these hastily affixed signs are often a symptom of poor planning and, possibly, library-centered rules. Usually, they are put in place because something isn't working very well. For example:

- Instructions for the self-check machine are taped next to the monitor because members have a difficult time using it.
- A regulatory sign is erected because the library hasn't balanced the competing needs for active and quiet space.
- A paper directional sign is needed to lead people to the meeting room because permanent signage is inadequate or nonexistent.

Assessing and Scoring

If you've conducted a signage audit as described in checkpoint 6.2 ("All signage uses the same visual language"), you'll have recorded whether your library is plagued with these signs or not. If it isn't, you've earned 10 points. If there are even a few paper signs taped up, 0 points.

Improving Your Score: Eliminating Taped-Up Paper Signs

The best way to address the problem of paper signs is to address the deeper problems that make the signs necessary. You could replace a paper sign with a professional one, sure, but it might just be window dressing. Fixing the root causes of these signs will not only clean up the visual environment, it will improve the way things work and make your library more pleasant to use.

6.6 Regulatory Signs Are Written in a Plain, Polite, and Friendly Manner

Why This Is Important   DIFFICULTY RATING: ★

Let's face it: libraries can get nasty when writing regulatory signs. And we know it won't be a stretch for you to agree that mean signs and the impolite messages they convey don't enhance members' experiences.

If you've been following along in order, you've already removed most or all of the regulatory signs in your library since they don't apply to most folks anyway and they're not effective. If you must have signs that state rules, make sure your library doesn't come off sounding or looking like a jerk.

Assessing Your Library

Use your signage audit to find all of the remaining regulatory signs in your library. Test the tone of these signs: if it's not something you would say in a face-to-face interaction with a library member, it's not something you should put on a sign. Look for any negative language. Is there a better way to communicate? If so, take note and schedule it for a rewrite.

Scoring

You get 10 points if all of your regulatory signs are plain, polite, and friendly. You get 5 points if 50 percent of them need improvement, and 0 points if more than 50 percent need help.

Improving Your Score: Rewriting Signs

This shouldn't take long because you've already removed most of the regulatory signs in your library. You have, haven't you?

Let's do a rewrite here to illustrate how you can take a bad sign and make it good. First, a sign that does *not* pass our tone test as described above: figure 6.7. It's mean. It's ugly. It's attempting to regulate behavior by regulating technology use. It's all around misguided, and it's poor communication. All of this detracts from creating a positive user experience.

fig. 6.7 Off-putting sign.

For a better solution, see figure 6.8. Notice that it no longer addresses technology. It deals with behavior. And it does so in a positive, uplifting manner.

Niceville Public Library

Polite use of cellphones encouraged!

fig. 6.8
Friendly sign.

6.7 Library Cards Contain Useful Information and Employ the Library's Visual Language

Why This Is Important

DIFFICULTY RATING: ★

Okay, we admit that this is an icing-on-the-cake type of checkpoint. Having an awesome library card design won't magically turn your library into a place that provides an amazing user experience. But still, don't forget about this piece of your visual identity. The library card is a representation of the library that members look at quite a bit, so make sure it is useful. A good library card is a small kindness, to be sure, but it's a kindness nevertheless.

Assessing and Scoring

Your card either employs your library's visual language or it doesn't. That's easy to assess. What about the card's content? Check to make sure it features the following information:

- library name
- library telephone number
- library hours
- library URL
- library address

- library slogan
- member name
- barcode

Give yourself up to 5 points depending on how great your library card design is.

Improving Your Score: Redesigning Your Library Card

Use the guidelines in your brand manual to inform the design of your card. If you're looking for some inspiration, take a look at some nicely designed business cards—there are plenty of galleries to browse online.

If you're going to design a new card, you may as well design a few different ones. Designing different cards can be as simple as using some of the different colors listed in your brand manual. Let library members choose the one they like best.

Also consider offering different size options. Some members might prefer a small loyalty card (or keytag) version instead of the classic credit card size.

6.8 First-Time Visitors Can Easily Locate All Parts of the Library

Why This Is Important   DIFFICULTY RATING: ★ ★

Making a good first impression is important, sure. But this checkpoint is about more than that. Because even longtime library members are like first-time visitors when they come to the library for a new task. Ensuring that a new visitor can easily locate all parts of the library will guarantee that all library users have an easy time navigating your building.

Assessing Your Library

Find some people that have never visited your library. Put them at the library's entrance and ask them to find some things. Present them with typical library use scenarios and watch what they do. These scenarios could include such tasks as

- Return a library item.
- Find the storytime room.
- Do research about a company.
- Pick up a reserved item.
- Find a staff member to ask a question.

Hang back and shadow them as they work out the tasks, observing them along the way. Do they wander blindly until they complete the task? Do they talk to any librarians? Do any librarians talk to them? Do they consult any signs? Where are their decision points (i.e., where they stop to make a decision about where to go next)? Do they not see a sign that could help them complete the task?

This is classic journey mapping (see chapter 2), and it can be extremely useful in helping you understand the various ways in which different people accomplish the same task and how long it takes them to do so.

> **Tip**
> Don't cheat and ask a librarian from the next town over to be your tester. Librarians know too much about libraries to behave like typical library members. Friends or relatives of library employees are fair game, though ideally you should select some people from the database of testers you've developed.

After your volunteers have completed their tasks, conduct a mini user interview by inquiring directly about their experiences. Ask what they thought was helpful and what was confusing. Together with your observations and the resulting journey map, you now have a lot of valuable data about what it takes to find your way around the library.

Scoring

If everyone completes their tasks quickly, easily, and without confusion, excellent. You've no work to do, and you've earned 15 points. If a lot of people had trouble finding parts of the library, you get 0 points.

Improve Your Score: Fixing Building Navigation Problems

If you notice that multiple people have trouble finding a certain place in the library, consider ways that you can make this place easier to find. Implement your best idea and run a few more tests. Did your change help? If not, iterate and test again until you get it right.

6.9 Additional Reading

GEL: Global Experience Language, BBC, www.bbc.co.uk/gel

Grid Systems in Graphic Design, by Josef Müller-Brockman (Ram Publications, 1996), www.amazon.com/dp/3721201450

*Identify: Basic Principles of Identity Design in the Iconic Trademarks of Chermayeff &
Geismar*, by Ivan Chermayeff, Tom Geismar, and Sagi Haviv, edited by Aaron
Kenedi (HOW Books, 2011), www.amazon.com/dp/1440310327

Learning Space Toolkit, http://learningspacetoolkit.org

The Non-Designer's Design Book, 3rd ed., by Robin Williams (Peachpit Press, 2008),
www.amazon.com/dp/B00125MJYM

*Signage and Wayfinding Design: A Complete Guide to Creating Environmental
Graphic Design Systems*, by Chris Calori (Wiley, 2007), www.amazon.com/
dp/0471748919

The Wayfinding Handbook: Information Design for Public Places, by David Gibson
(Princeton Architectural Press, 2009), www.amazon.com/dp/1568987692

Chapter 7

Online Presence

▶ **THERE'S A GOOD CHANCE THAT MORE PEOPLE VISIT YOUR WEBSITE THAN** visit your building. Is the effort you spend on your website commensurate with the amount of attention your members give it? Probably not. If you're ready to take stock of your library's online presence, this chapter is for you. In this chapter, we help you get a handle on your website and realign it so that it better serves your members.

7.1 Members Can Easily Search for Library Items and Place Holds

Why This Is Important   DIFFICULTY RATING: ★ ★ ★

Have you ever searched Amazon to pull together basic bibliographic information before heading into your library's OPAC (online public access catalog)? Yeah, us too. If *we* think our discovery systems can be a drag, how must library members feel?

It is a really big deal that our catalogs are difficult to use. Why? The vast majority of people use our websites for one purpose: to find, renew, and reserve items. Above most everything else, your library should make this really easy to do. It is a major critical task! Just ask a few people in your library why they visit your website and see what they say. We bet you'll hear a lot about searching for items.

It's easy enough to put a search box front and center on your home page (and to make one available on every page), but unfortunately that's where our control over the experience usually ends. After conducting a search, users are whisked away to a completely different and often difficult-to-use environment.

The importance of discovery and our lack of control over the experience puts libraries in a bad place.

Assessing and Scoring

While you can ask people their opinion about finding, renewing, and reserving items, the best way to learn what sort of experiences members are having with your catalog is to conduct some usability tests. Only by observing them will you be able to find out where folks are getting tripped up using your catalog.

Draft a usability test that asks questions that address the major functionality of your catalog. Try these questions (or variations that work for your local environment):

1. Your fourteen-year-old has taken up parkour and you'd like to find out more about it. Find three books on the topic that are currently in the library and available to be borrowed.
2. You're interested in the latest vegan cookbook by Alicia Silverstone. Search the library catalog and place a hold on it.
3. You've borrowed three books from the library and they are all overdue. Renew them.

Use the instructions that we outline in checkpoint 7.2 ("Members can easily accomplish critical tasks") to conduct your usability test. Score 10 points if most of your testers were able to complete the test successfully, 5 points if the results were split evenly, and 0 points if most of your testers were unsuccessful in completing the three tasks.

Improving Your Score: Improving the Discovery Experience

For the most part, libraries buy OPACs from vendors. And while some vendors put effort into designing good interfaces by using user-centered design and testing techniques, not all do. Libraries have very little input into the design process and, therefore, little to no control over the end results. We might be able to make some improvements by editing stylesheets or employing the odd JavaScript workarounds, but we can only do so much.

So we either have to get creative or we need to forgo the out-of-the-box catalog interface that ships with our ILSs (integrated library systems). Sometimes our creative options are limited, but we've seen a few libraries have some success with using third-party tools to expose certain types of content from their collections—for example, putting their new books into an application like LibraryThing (www.librarything .com) or Goodreads (www.goodreads.com) and using one of the display options those tools provide to display new titles on their home pages in slick cover-flow widgets. While solutions such as these don't do anything to *fix* the poor catalog experience, they might help improve browsing and discovery of library collections.

If you want to make large-scale changes to your catalog, you'll have to use a discovery layer overlay. Major options include Blacklight (http://projectblacklight .org), BiblioCommons (www.bibliocommons.com), SOPAC (http://thesocialopac.net), and VuFind (http://vufind.org). These pieces of software allow libraries to continue to use the back ends of their ILSs while creating a more usable skin for the front end. Since you won't have to migrate ILSs to use an overlay, it isn't as daunting a task as it could be if you were implementing a whole new ILS/catalog.

7.2 Members Can Easily Accomplish Critical Tasks

DIFFICULTY RATING: ★

Remember the last time you visited your online banking website and got distracted by the list of events at local branches? And how about that retirement date calculator? And that annotated list of exciting new mutual funds? If you've never experienced such distractions, there's a good reason for that: your bank has decided to simplify the online banking experience for their clients because they know that when they visit the site, it's to get something done, not to browse around to see what's new or what's happening. That's what this checkpoint is all about: we want to help you figure out what people want to do on your website so that you can ensure that they're having an easy time doing those things. It is essential to the entire enterprise of having a website. Skip it at your site's peril!

Why This Is Important

People visit your library's website because they're on a mission. That mission is probably different depending on the visitor: perhaps he wants to know when he can bring his toddler for a storytime, or maybe he needs to renew an overdue book.

Some of these tasks are really important. For instance, searching for an item is central to the purpose of using a library and library website. Other tasks—looking for the library's email address is a good example—are very common. Paying attention to these important and common needs is the only way you can make your library website useful. Accordingly, these critical tasks should be the primary focus of your web efforts. Does your site facilitate the completion of these critical tasks?

Assessing Your Library

In order to determine whether your members can easily accomplish critical tasks, you'll need to do two things:

1. Figure out what these critical tasks are
2. Conduct usability tests on your site

Determining Critical Tasks

Library websites often have a lot of different content. How can we determine the critical tasks for our sites? The easy way: ask our members.

INFORMAL INTERVIEWS Because people using the library are likely to be library website users, you won't have a difficult time finding people to interview. All you have to do is walk out of your office and start talking to people. You won't take up much of their time since you have only one question. Ask them, "Why do you use the library's website?" Record their first few answers and thank them for their time. It won't take many interviews for you to see patterns develop, but make sure you interview people in different areas of the library. You'll be sure to get data from different types of library users. We recommend you interview ten to fifteen people in each department.

After these interviews, rank the responses according to frequency. The tasks that rise to the top are the critical ones. Your site must do these things well in order for people to be successful using it.

WEB ANALYTICS In addition to asking people about what they do on your site, take a look at your site analytics. Your analytics will tell you what people are *actually doing* on your site. There's a chance that what people say they do on your site and what they're actually doing are slightly different! Compare the data and if your analytics tell you there's some frequently accessed content that people didn't report using, add it to your list of critical tasks.

Usability Testing

Knowing your site's critical tasks is a great first step, but don't stop now. Next you should ensure that these things are easy for people to do. There's only one way to do this: conduct some usability tests.

Usability tests are so important because we see our sites differently than our users see our sites. While it is possible for librarians to have useful insights about their websites, generally we're too knowledgeable about libraries—and too immersed in the creation of our sites—to consistently make objective observations that lead to improvements. Usability testing lets us set aside our biases and witness how novices perceive and use our sites.

Beyond critical tasks

Thinking about critical tasks is very useful, but delving a bit deeper and examining people's motivations can also help us design our sites better.

What Is a Usability Test?

A usability test is a research technique in which a product's end user is observed using the product. In the case of a website, the observer watches someone use the website. So to test your library website you'd watch someone accomplish—or try to accomplish—common library tasks. In the process, you'll learn where your site is giving people troubles and what you can do to make it easier to use your site.

Planning for Usability Tests

Conducting usability tests is a straightforward activity, but your sessions will benefit from some planning. Here's how to plan for an afternoon of testing.

FIND FIVE TESTERS Good news: you can use almost anyone for your usability tests. The only people we recommend you avoid using are library workers and people with absolutely no web experience. Library workers know too much about libraries to be objective testers, and a complete web novice's lack of skills will get in the way of testing. Otherwise, pretty much anyone is okay. They can be library users or non-users, and they can have a range of experience with the web. You can recruit people that are in the library, put an ad on Craigslist, or enlist some friends. Collect their contact information and remind them about the test a week or a few days before the big day.

DEVELOP SCENARIOS During your usability tests you'll be asking people to carry out tasks. The language you use to do this is very important because it can influence their behavior. Let's pretend that using library databases is a critical task and you want to see if people are successful in their attempts. Your initial reaction might be to ask of someone, "Okay now, please search for an article using our databases." Three of those words—"search," "article," and "databases"—might constitute too much information and give people clues about what to do.

Instead of giving people literal instructions, you should present fictional scenarios to them. Here's a scenario that would work to test people's use of the library's article databases:

> You're in the process of training for your first marathon. You heard a story on the radio about some new research doctors have done into long-distance running, and you want to know more. Use the library's resources to see if you can find this new research.

Scenarios prevent your prompts from leading people and will result in a more realistic test.

When conducting tests you'll have a list of these scenarios to read from. You should also give your testers a piece of paper with the main prompt from each scenario in case they need a reminder.

WRITE A SCRIPT Following a script takes the guesswork out of conducing a usability test. After greeting a tester—be sure to establish a friendly rapport—all you'll have to do is read what you've already written. Ensuring that all site testers hear the same instructions will bring rigor to your testing, resulting in more valuable data in the end.

An essential part of the script is making your testers feel comfortable. Remember, they might be concerned about being judged for their inability to complete tasks or they might just feel self-conscious. Be explicit about the purpose of the session—to test the library's site, not them. Remind them that they shouldn't be concerned with making mistakes because there are no mistakes they can make. Give them permission to say whatever's on their mind about the site and to not be concerned with hurting anyone's feelings.

SET UP A ROOM Your room setup needn't be elaborate, but you should make sure you have a quiet, distraction-free space to conduct your tests. An office, a cubicle, or even a quiet spot in the library should work well. Avoid conducting your tests with laptops since some people might not be accustomed to working on them. Instead, provide a standard keyboard and mouse. If you have computers running Microsoft Windows and Apple's OS X, set them both up and give people the chance to use their operating system of choice.

This is all the room setup and hardware you need to conduct a usability test. If you want to have other library employees observe the tests, you'll need to set up a microphone and screen-sharing software, too.

Conducting Usability Tests

WHAT TO RECORD While conducting the test, keep track of the task completion rate. You can also record subjective notes about where people got tripped up, any quick thoughts about how to prevent this from happening, and anything interesting that testers say while they're using your site.

You might choose to record all of the tests with screencasting software like ScreenFlow (www.telestream.net/screenflow/overview.htm), but it isn't necessary. If you do, reviewing the test videos will take at least double the time it took to conduct the test. In the end, you might be better off devoting that time to another round of usability testing rather than focusing so intently on one that just happened. But if you've never conducted a usability test before and think you'll miss some important information, recording the test might make you feel more comfortable.

WHO OBSERVES THE USABILITY TEST? If your library's site isn't a political battleground, and you just want to learn how you can improve it, you don't need to involve anyone else in the testing process. You can observe, learn, make changes, and repeat.

But usability tests can do more than clue you in on website issues. They can help you educate stakeholders and manage their expectations. Having library administration watch people use the site can help you make the case for increased funding and staffing. It can also help move conversations from people talking about their own ideas and preferences to talking about user behavior. Consider inviting the appropriate folks to observe the tests if you want to get some buy-in for making changes.

If you do want others to see the tests, don't crowd everyone into the testing room. It will be difficult for everyone to see what's going on, and it can be intimidating for the tester. Instead, use screen-sharing software like join.me (https://join .me) to project the test elsewhere. Or, host a viewing party of the recorded tests.

REPORTING RESULTS If people in your library are watching the tests live, don't delay the discussion. Schedule a same-day meeting so that details are fresh in everyone's mind.

If you're doing the testing just for the results, you can write up a summary of what you learned and pass it on to interested parties.

TEST EARLY AND OFTEN Don't just test once and be done with it. Ideally, you'll get into a routine of conducting tests, fixing problems, and retesting. This type of continual, incremental improvement is good for staff morale, and good for library members.

Scoring

What was the completion rate for your test? Could all of your testers complete all of the tasks? Did most testers have trouble with a certain task? Scoring this checkpoint will be a bit subjective. If you're overall pleased with how your site performed, give yourself 20 points. If there's a lot of stuff to be improved, you get less than 10 points.

Tip

If you're designing a new website or otherwise thinking about making changes to your site, you don't have to wait until the changes are live to conduct some usability tests. Testing prototypes is a fantastic way to save time and iron out kinks before members get frustrated.

Testing prototypes can fit in no matter what your design and development process is. If you're mocking up pages in code, great—use those for some tests. But don't forget that it can be just as effective to use Photoshop mockups or even sketches made on paper. For more on this form of usability testing, see *Paper Prototyping*, by Carolyn Snyder (Morgan Kaufmann, 2003).

7.3 The Size of Your Website Is Commensurate with the Amount of Effort You Can Devote to It

Why This Is Important

DIFFICULTY RATING: ★

It is easy to create a new page on a website. It only takes a fraction of a second. Filling that page with appropriately written content, an attractive image, and then maintaining it all? That takes a lot more effort. We've seen a lot of libraries that become infatuated with creating many, many pages on their websites. With many different departments all wanting or even demanding to have a presence on the library website, it is easy to see why new pages or sub-sites get created. But like most infatuations, these pages rarely enjoy any follow-through in the long term. They're left to languish while attention is given to the next exciting thing. This results in a website full of half-baked, marginal content. Instead of short flings with meaningless content, develop relationships with content that's truly important.

We're advocating here for library websites that are small. The smaller your website is, the more attention you'll be able to give each individual bit of content. Don't spread your efforts thin. Reducing the number of pages you need to maintain will free up your time so you can concentrate on the remaining, important pages.

The more content you have, the more design decisions you'll have to make. Each additional decision is an opportunity to make a mistake. Groups of content end up in different sections and require increasingly sophisticated architecture, labeling, navigation, and visual design. It isn't impossible to get all of these things right, but more often than not people feel like they're trying to find a needle in a haystack. Making that haystack smaller will make it easier for people to find what they want.

In fact, it is entirely reasonable to decide that your haystack should be quite small. It would be better to have a library website with no additional content beyond what is needed to support critical tasks than it would be to have a website filled with irrelevant content.

Assessing Your Library

Just how small your website should be depends on both the size of your web team and the current status of your website. In checkpoint 7.4 ("Web content is engaging"), you'll be conducting a content audit. You can use that to judge the overall quality of your site. How many pages received a bunch of 1s or 0s? If even a quarter of your pages need serious improvement, your web team is spread too thin. Remedy this by hiring more people or reducing the number of pages on your site. Given the condition of most library budgets, the second option is probably more realistic. It may even be preferable. Remember: on the web, less is more. Or, as we prefer to say, *less is less*, and that's okay. In fact, it's awesome.

Scoring

Is your site the right size? You get 10 points. Is it huge and sprawling and there's not enough staff to do the work? Give yourself 0 points.

Improving Your Score: Reducing the Size of Your Site

What should you keep? What should you cut? These are big questions, but paring down website content doesn't have to be challenging. In this discussion, it is useful to think about your content as a balance of what members want to do on the site, what the library wants to include on the site, and what the library's organizational capacity will allow.

MEMBER NEEDS These are the site's critical tasks. See checkpoint 7.2 ("Members can easily accomplish critical tasks") for a discussion of critical tasks and how to determine what they are. Don't cut any critical tasks.

LIBRARY NEEDS In most libraries, staff from many different departments have content requests. If there's no process in place for evaluating them, it can be difficult to deal with these requests in a productive manner; staff can get frustrated, and web librarians can easily feel overwhelmed. A bad situation for everyone! Most of the time, content gets added and library sites accumulate nonstrategic content. To avoid this, develop a content strategy that everyone understands. Having clear rules for what sort of library content the website will support moves the conversation from staff demanding or begging that their opinions be heard to everyone thinking about how they can support the overall purpose of the website.

ORGANIZATIONAL CAPACITY Assessing just how much work your web team can do will help you determine how much content you need to cut. Perhaps your library has enough capacity to adequately maintain fifty pages. Perhaps only twenty-five. Err on the side of small. If, after cutting pages, your web team has everything under control and is sitting around killing time by watching YouTube, then it might be time to consider adding some pages back.

MOBILE FIRST Another way to brainstorm the most important parts of your website is to imagine you're building a mobile version. Given the limited screen real estate available, what parts of your site are essential? This list will probably be very similar to your list of critical tasks.

ANALYTICS Your site's analytics might also help, but they can be tricky to interpret. Page hits don't tell us much about motivation for visiting pages. They might get skipped either because the content isn't interesting or because something is hampering findability and usability. While a lack of visits doesn't necessarily mean a page isn't valuable, it does mean that it probably won't be missed. Use these stats judiciously. Once you've determined the most important things to have on your site, consider the rest nice to have but not necessary.

WHEN IN DOUBT, CUT IT OUT! If you're not sure about the utility of a piece of content, get rid of it. If it turns out to be an important piece of content and people start missing it, they'll pipe up. You can always add it back, but we bet you won't have to.

7.4 Web Content Is Engaging

Why This Is Important   DIFFICULTY RATING: ★ ★

The truth is, the stuff you have on your website is why people visit it. The content is the very reason your site exists. Accordingly, your library needs to take its website content very seriously. Not only does the content need to be appropriately written and formatted for the web, the substance of the content needs to be relevant to members' needs.

We've been working with library websites for a lot of years, and while we're happy to see a general improvement in the way libraries plan and develop their web presences, library website content still causes us some consternation. Many libraries seem to have figured out that things like navigation, search, and findability are all important, but those same libraries treat content planning, development, and management as an afterthought. We even know of a number of large, well-funded libraries that devote entire departments to web development (complete with developers, interface designers, and usability experts) but leave content to other library staff, without the coordination and guidance necessary to ensure that this content meets standards and best practices. Bad idea. Populating your website with engaging and relevant content doesn't happen magically or by accident. It takes some serious planning.

While we fully agree that the structure, architecture, and design of a website are crucial, we also believe that the words and images on the page are just as important. It does your members no good to have a perfectly and intuitively designed website if the content on that site doesn't meet their needs. Think of it this way: would you read a magazine that's dedicated to the history of chainsaws? Probably not. Even if this magazine were well written and filled with beautiful photographs, it wouldn't hold your interest for very long. There's no amount of visual design and clear writing that could make this subject interesting for you. Likewise, it doesn't matter how pretty or well written your website is if the content isn't interesting to the folks in your community.

Assessing Your Library

We wish we could give you an easy rubric for assessing the content on your site. Unfortunately, it's not as simple as making sure your site has pictures of cute puppies and the local weather. It's a bit more complicated because different communities have different content needs. The good news is that there's a straightforward way to examine your site and see if the content is worthwhile.

Content Audit

The purpose of a content audit is to take stock of what's on your website and critically evaluate it. This evaluation process will help you determine what content you need to improve, what you can cut, and what you might need to add. And that's not all! You'll see that there are many different aspects of your content you can evaluate in an audit.

In a content audit you'll review *every piece of content* on your site. Not only every page, but also PDFs, audio and video files, and whatever else you might have lying around. This can be a daunting task, so if your library's site is huge, consider enlisting help from folks around the library who contribute to the website. A content audit is a collection of metadata about your site, so if you like cataloging, you'll love content audits.

Conducting an Audit

The audit will be housed in a spreadsheet like the one in figure 7.1. The first things you'll record are quantitative in nature:

- Page ID
- URL
- Page name
- File type

	A	B	C
1	**PAGE ID**	**URL**	**NAME**
2	1.0	http:uxlibrary.org	home page
3	1.1	http:uxlibrary.org/research	Research
4	1.2	http:uxlibrary.org/reading	Reading
5	1.3	http:uxlibrary.org/cafe	Library Cafe
6	1.2.1	http:uxlibrary.org/reading/comics	Comic Books
7	1.2.2	http:uxlibrary.org/reading/classics	Classics

fig. 7.1 Content audit.

The real benefit comes when you take the time to record some qualitative information. For the purpose of assessing its relevance, examine and rate the following three aspects of your content.

USEFUL TO MEMBERS Adopt your users' perspective when analyzing, and ask yourself, "What need is this content filling for website users? Who would miss it if it were removed?" Be honest, brutally honest if need be, when doing this. Don't inflate the score just because you think this content could maybe, possibly, come in handy for someone at some point. Use what you know about your site's critical tasks and your community's interests when assigning a score.

USEFUL TO LIBRARY Is this piece of content important for the library to have online? Would anything bad happen if this content were removed?

USE How much traffic is the page getting? Create a rating scale for each aspect of the content, and keep it narrow. For instance, the scale for "useful to members" and "useful to library" could be

0—Not at all useful
1—Somewhat useful
2—Essential

A rating scale for "use" could be

0—< 1,000 hits per month
1—1,001 to 5,000 hits per month
2—> 5,001 hits per month

Scoring

It should be pretty obvious to you that a content audit is not a quick and easy process. It will take the time and commitment of a number of people (the bigger your site, the greater the time and commitment from more people!), but we promise it's worth the effort. For the purposes of scoring this checkpoint, give yourself 10 points if more than 75 percent of your site content scores on the high end of all three aspects: useful to members, useful to library, use; 5 points if your content is in the 50 percent range; and 0 points if less than 50 percent of your content scores well on all three.

Improving Your Score: Analyzing Your Content

Once you've ranked these aspects of your content, you can sort the columns in your spreadsheet to find out some interesting things. What percentage of your content received a 0 or 1 for "useful to members"? What's the most popular content on your site? What content is being ignored? If you discover some content that isn't very useful and is receiving little traffic, remove it. No one will miss it! If you discover content that's truly useful but is receiving little traffic, consider ways to make it easier to find.

Using the results of your content audit in this way, you can instantly see how exposing the weaknesses of your content gives you an instant plan for improving it. As with most forms of user research, your first pass through your content shouldn't be your last. It's important to work this sort of content evaluation into your regular content maintenance workflow. So, for example, when one of your content contributors updates a page or adds new content, you should apply these same evaluative questions to the updated/new content so that it gets reviewed in the same way as the rest of the content on your site. This will also ensure that your site won't eventually fall victim to the seemingly inevitable content bloat that every website manager fears, dreads, and loses sleep over.

Scoping your content

Before you create a bunch of content for your site, make sure to heed the advice from checkpoint 7.3 in this chapter. Your members will be better off having a small amount of content that supports the things they want to do rather than a large amount of less-focused content.

Making the Most of Your Content Audit

To round out your knowledge, you can also evaluate other aspects of your content. Here are some suggestions:

Written for the web

Is the writing as concise, easy to scan, and friendly as can be?

Current

When was the content last updated?

Accurate

Is the information correct?

You can use this additional information to do some additional sorting of columns. For instance, make sure all of your popular content is both accurate and written for the web (see next checkpoint).

7.5 Content Is Written for the Web

Why This Is Important
DIFFICULTY RATING: ★

If your library has a website, it is in the publishing business. Accordingly, you need to take the writing on your website very seriously. This shouldn't come as a surprise. After all, the content on your site is the very reason people are using it. Since it's so important, we think it's worth taking the time to expertly craft it.

What's so special about writing for the web? A few things, the most important of which is that crafting content for the web needs to take into account people's web-reading behaviors. People are often on a mission when they're using the web. They need a piece of information, or they're hoping to accomplish a task. And they want to accomplish their mission as soon as possible. So instead of reading every word on a page, they tend to ready quickly and scan. We should make sure our websites facilitate this reading behavior.

You don't have to wait until you're developing new pages to write web-appropriate content. Rewriting existing content is an extremely effective way to give your site a makeover.

Assessing and Scoring

Writing for the web doesn't happen automatically or naturally. If you've never comprehensively rewritten your site's content, you get 0 points. You can earn all 10 points when you've rewritten all of your content.

Improving Your Score: Rewriting Content

Make changes to your most popular pages first, but be sure to follow up and rewrite all of your pages. If it isn't worth improving, it isn't worth having on your site.

Instead of rewriting a page by starting from scratch, edit it multiple times, improving one aspect with each pass. For instance, first **remove words**, then rearrange the content so that it employs an **inverted pyramid** style, then **rewrite links** as needed, and so on.

Use these guidelines to help you plan your editing process.

REMOVE WORDS The fewer words you use, the less readers will have to skip over. For starters, don't be afraid to use sentence fragments for smaller chunks of information. Here's an example:

Bad: Place a hold on an item.

Good: Reserve item

AVOID CLIPART AND STOCK PHOTOS At best these things add no value to a web page. At worst (and most often) these things are nothing but distracting clutter that make pages seem hectic. If you're going to use photographs, make sure they're high quality and authentic.

USE THE INVERTED PYRAMID After reducing the amount of stuff on a page, you can reorder what's left for maximum effectiveness. While librarians might be accustomed to writing big introductions and narrowing down to a thesis for school papers, take the opposite approach when writing for the web.

Put the most important information at the top of a page's content area. That's where people are mostly likely to look, so putting the important information there increases the likelihood that they'll read it. It is a wasted opportunity to put introductory or welcome language at the top of a page because it conveys no value. Secondary details, background information, and other less important information can go to the bottom of the page.

USE HEADINGS Think of headings as labels for chunks of information. They save time by enabling readers to glean the content of a paragraph by reading just a few words. If a heading seems to indicate that the information will help them complete their mission, they will continue. If not, they will move on, scanning other headings until they find what they're looking for.

To be most effective, headings should be visually distinct from the information they describe. A good way to do this is to make them larger, bold, or possibly a different color. But beware of floating headers, which occur when the spacing between headers and content makes it unclear what chunk of information a header belongs to. In figure 7.2, compare the first column (bad) with the second (good).

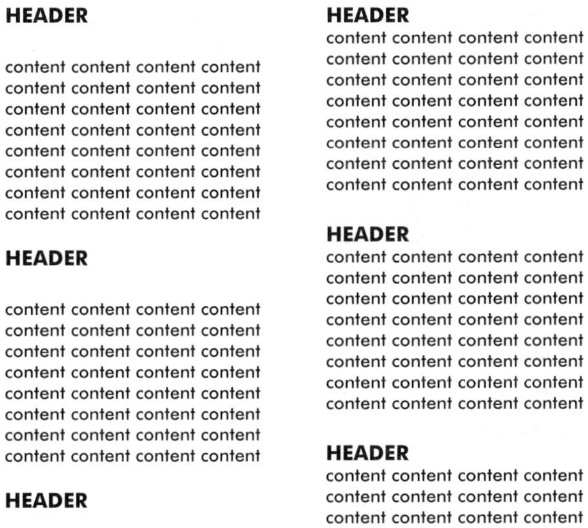

fig. 7.2
Heading and
content.

HEADER

content content content content
content content content content
content content content content
content content content content
content content content content
content content content content
content content content content
content content content content

HEADER

content content content content
content content content content
content content content content
content content content content
content content content content
content content content content
content content content content
content content content content

HEADER

HEADER

content content content content
content content content content
content content content content
content content content content
content content content content
content content content content
content content content content
content content content content

HEADER

content content content content
content content content content
content content content content
content content content content
content content content content
content content content content
content content content content
content content content content

HEADER

content content content content
content content content content
content content content content

WRITE DESCRIPTIVE LINKS Link text should be descriptive, active, not too long, and not too short. Here are some examples of what to avoid and what to aim for:

Avoid: To access your account, <u>click here</u>.

Okay: <u>Account</u>

Best: <u>Access your account</u>

USE BULLETED LISTS Like headings, bulleted lists help people scan. If you find any lists in paragraph form, consider breaking the items out in bullet points. Compare this paragraph:

To get a library card you must bring in a driver's license, state id, or a utility bill.

with this version, which uses a list:

To get a library card bring in one:
- driver's license
- state ID
- utility bill

AIM FOR A CONVERSATIONAL TONE When library members attempt to accomplish something on your website, they're entering into a conversation of sorts. They might say to themselves something like this:

- "What time does the library open on Saturday?"
- "I need to renew this DVD."
- "When is the next toddler storytime?"

To make your content easy to understand, make sure it responds in a similarly conversational way. An extremely effective way to do this is to anticipate the questions that members want to answer and use those as headings on a page. As they scan the page, they'll recognize a question as the one they're asking and know to read the information below. See figures 7.3 and 7.4 for the before and after versions, respectively, of a page that was rewritten to employ this technique.

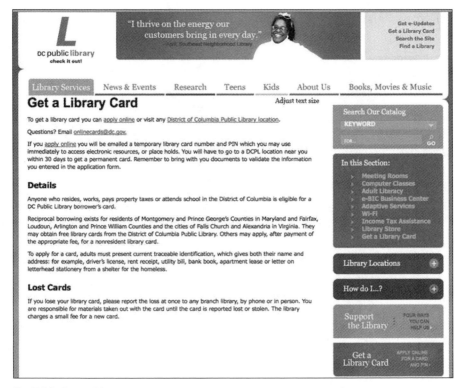

fig. 7.3 Before revision.

fig. 7.4 After revision.

Another surefire way to make your web content conversational is to avoid using the passive voice in favor of using the active voice as much as possible. It's easy to fall into the trap of using the passive voice because we tend to think that passively constructed phrases sound more authoritative than actively phrased ones. In truth, they just sound unfriendly and stilted. Compare:

Bad: Copies of the library's newsletter can be found on the About Us page.

Good: You can find copies of our newsletter on the About Us page.

AVOID JARGON Jargon is confusing, and it can make people feel stupid. It finds its way onto our websites because we're so steeped in our profession that we forget library members aren't. Put an end to this library-centered thinking and remove the jargon from your site. Plain language will make it easier for members to understand what you're trying to communicate.

To assess the language on your website, first see John Kupersmith's *Library Terms That Users Understand* (http://escholarship.org/uc/item/3qq499w7) for some initial perspective. Kupersmith's report details the results of usability tests that found that users don't understand terms like

- database
- library catalog
- e-journals
- reference
- resource
- any brand name (e.g., EBSCO)
- acronyms (e.g., ILL)

The report also suggests the kinds of terms that users do understand:

- find books
- services
- my library account

Reading Kupersmith's report is a good start, but don't use it to make any final decisions about the words you're employing. You'll get much better results by doing a little bit of testing yourself.

TEST LABELS You can do this formally, or you can spend a few afternoons going out into the stacks and asking some library members for a few moments of their time. Either way, the idea here is to show people your top-level navigation labels—one at a time—and ask them what types of things they'd expect to find in this category. Assure them that there are no right or wrong answers and that you're just interested in their honest opinions. Record their responses and compare what they expect versus what you're giving them.

DO SOME CARD SORTS Card sorts take the opposite approach. Instead of starting with labels and talking about content, present people with descriptions of content and instruct them to organize them into groups and assign labels. Refer to chapter 2, section 2.2, for a brief introduction to card sorting. When you're ready to perform a card sort on your site, your best bet is to place all your navigation items onto individual cards and have a few of your members sort those cards into groupings that make sense to them. Once they've done the sorting, get them to give a name to each of the groupings. This exercise tests your navigation scheme and gives you some insight into the kinds of terminology and labels that are meaningful to your members.

Once you've tested all of the navigation on your site and implemented changes, you'll still have some ongoing work to do. You can ensure the labels on your site remain user-centered by conducting a few small tests any time you're going to add something. If you're diligent about this, the next time you do a full test of your navigation it should be a breeze.

7.6 Website Employs Web Design Conventions

Why This Is Important   DIFFICULTY RATING: ★

When you're waiting at a traffic light, what color do you expect it to turn to signal that it is safe for you to go? Green, right? This is a convention employed in your town, in the neighboring towns, across the country, and in pretty much every country in the known universe that has traffic lights. If different towns chose different colors and designs for their traffic lights, the result would be chaos. Instead, everyone has agreed to standardize colors so that if you're familiar with one traffic light you're familiar with them all.

Likewise, there are tried-and-true website conventions that, whether they consciously realize it or not, people expect. Employing these conventions will make your library website environment familiar to web users. It will behave the way they expect it to behave. This will not only increase the usability of your site, it will also increase its trustworthiness.

Assessing Your Library

Check to make sure your site employs the following conventions. If it doesn't, getting it in line will be a relatively quick and easy way to improve your site.

SITE LOGO Your library's name or logo should appear in the upper left of the browser on every page of your site. Whether it is text or an image file it should also be a link to your home page. This serves as a surefire navigation trick for users. If they get lost browsing your site, they expect to be able to start over by clicking your logo at the top left.

LINKS Make hyperlinks visually distinct from other text on your site. For textual links, this is best accomplished by assigning a different color and underlining them.

The most conservative and perhaps old-fashioned convention is to make them blue (the earliest web browsers did this out of the box, so it's something people began to expect). Other colors can also work, provided that they are sufficiently different from the plain text on your site and contrast enough with the site's background color. If you've decided to go with blue, remember that no other text on the site should be blue other than links. You want your links to stand out as clickable, so if other, non-clickable text on your site is also blue, you've lost the battle. Don't forget to also assign a different color to links that people have already visited. This will help orient them further. Ideally, the color of your visited links will be a muted version of the color you've chosen for unvisited links.

For related information about writing links, see checkpoint 7.5 ("Content is written for the web").

BREADCRUMBS Your site's main navigation isn't the only way people orient themselves on your website. Breadcrumbs are additional navigational tools that often appear at the top of a web page's main content area. The most common type of breadcrumbs are location breadcrumbs that show the location of a page in a site's hierarchal structure. Breadcrumbs orient website users and provide an alternative way to navigate your site.

The other kind of breadcrumb trail that's sometimes used on websites is a path-based trail. Path-based breadcrumb trails indicate the path the user took to get to

> Home / About / **Library Policies**

the current page. This style of breadcrumb is rarely used anymore, and we recommend avoiding it.

If your site is large, make sure you provide breadcrumbs. If your site doesn't have a deep hierarchal structure and has only one or two levels, you can probably get away without using breadcrumbs.

CONTACT AND LOCATION INFO A lot of people visit your site looking for a phone number or an address. Make sure they don't have to spend a lot of time hunting for it. Good options include

- adding a top-level navigation item labeled "Contact" or "Contact & Locations"

- including the information in the site's banner at the top right of the browser
- repeating this information in the page's footer

SEARCH Having the ability to search your website is a convention that most web users simply expect. Make sure your site search features prominently and in the same place on every page on your site—somewhere in your navigation bar or at the top of every page is a likely place users probably expect to see a search option. The complicating factor for library websites is that your members might see a search box and expect to be able to use it to search the library's holdings in addition to website content. If your site and catalog are well integrated and searchable from a single search box, kudos to you! If they aren't, you could include two radio buttons below your search box, one to search the site and the other to search the catalog.

CONSISTENT NAVIGATION THROUGHOUT THE SITE Just like when they're in your physical building, when someone is using your website they should know where they are, what they can do, and how to move around successfully. Consistent website navigation is important because it helps users stay oriented.

Oftentimes library website navigation becomes inconsistent because separate blogs or micro sites are tacked on to main sites. These separate websites usually have different visual designs and navigational schemes. When users click from one interface only to see a completely different one, they might get confused and disoriented. These feelings reduce confidence—in themselves and the site—and hinder their progress accomplishing tasks.

Unfortunately, piecemeal site building is common because it is the easy way to add major pieces of new content to a site. Instead of taking the time to examine how new content fits into the larger purpose—and organizational structure—of the site, it is quicker to create something new and link to it.

The library catalog is another element that is usually visually distinct from the rest of a library's website. Here, too, the transition from one navigational scheme to another can be disorienting. A few libraries have done something about this situation. Check out the websites from the Darien Library (www.darienlibrary.org) and the Topeka and Shawnee County Public Library (http://tscpl.org) for examples of a catalog experience that's tightly integrated into the rest of the web experience.

REDUCING NAVIGATIONAL SCHEMES If you're exposing your members to more than one navigational scheme and want to simplify things, you'll either have to cut extraneous content or fold it into your main site. Aside from large special collections or distinct projects, if something isn't important enough to be folded into your main navigational scheme, it isn't worth having at all. Consider getting rid of the content if you can't find a way to include it in your main navigation.

Scoring

Give yourself 10 points if your site employs the majority of these conventions. Half of the conventions? You get 5 points. Very few? Give yourself 0 points.

Improving Your Score: Employing Web Design Conventions

Use the information in the assessment section as a guide. Change your site so that it follows the guidelines discussed there.

7.7 Home Page Clearly Expresses What People Can Do on Your Site

Why This Is Important   DIFFICULTY RATING: ★ ★

People on the web are impatient and tend to make snap judgments about the value of a website. Making sure your home page tells the right story is an effective way to shape how people judge your site. Your home page can tell people, "This is what we're all about" and, "Here's what you can accomplish on this site." This conveys the value of your site while building user confidence.

A well-crafted home page does more than influence people's perceptions. It also increases a site's usability by leading people in the directions that they want to go. And since usability is a necessary component for creating a good user experience, it follows that home page design is a user experience issue.

Let's look at a few library home pages to see how they impact a user's experience.

fig. 7.5 Cambridge Public Library home page.

CAMBRIDGE LIBRARIES AND GALLERIES (HTTPS://CAMBRIDGELIBRARIES.CA)

Figure 7.5 shows an extremely visually striking page. The image is fresh, the branding is striking, and the overall impression you get from this home page is that the library is a vibrant place. Unfortunately, that's about all that this home page does. While it is nice that there are only four main navigation items on this page, that isn't the whole story. The "Main Menu" label hides the site's full navigational structure. The fact that this requires users to make an extra click isn't as harmful as the fact that it prevents people from instantly knowing what they can do on the site.

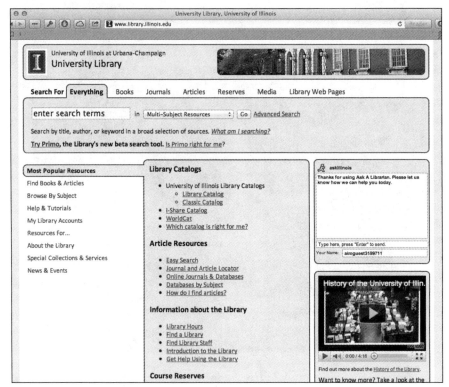

fig. 7.6 University of Illinois Library home page.

UNIVERSITY OF ILLINOIS AT URBANA-CHAMPAIGN LIBRARY (WWW.LIBRARY.UIUC.EDU)

Figure 7.6 shows a troubled home page that obscures the site's purpose by providing too many options. So while the page is certainly expressing what people can do on the site, it is not doing so clearly. Somewhere among all of those links are some useful options, but they're muted by the presence of everything else. The page would be better if instead it highlighted the availability of the most important tasks.

MONTANA STATE UNIVERSITY LIBRARY (WWW.LIB.MONTANA.EDU)

Figure 7.7 shows a page that is visually appealing, and it expresses a conservative, academic feeling. It also offers users options for action. The prominently displayed navigation labels are easy to understand: "Find," "Request," and "Help." There's also an easy-to-see search box. This home page is free from clutter and gets people where they want to go. We like this one a lot.

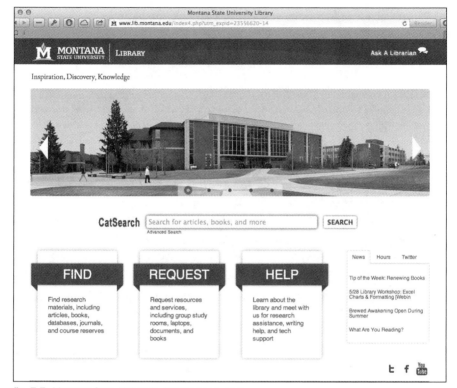

fig. 7.7 Montana State University Library home page.

Assessing Your Library

A great way to determine if your home page is letting people know what they can do on the site is to conduct some five-second tests (introduced in chapter 2). A five-second test is a type of usability test in which testers look at a web page for, you guessed it, five seconds. They're then asked to recall what they saw on the page.

When you conduct five-second tests to assess what your home page is communicating, be careful about the questions you ask your testers. Don't start by asking, "What can you do on this page?" It's too leading. Instead, ask, "What do you remember about this page?" Maybe you'll hear about the colors they remember, or maybe you'll hear about certain pictures or words. If people actually describe some of the things that can be done on your site, great! That's a sure sign your page is effectively communicating.

Only when a tester seems to have run out of responses to your initial question should you ask the follow-up: "What can you do on this page?" It is okay to lead them now.

Record all of your testers' responses and look for patterns. Reviewing the responses should clue you in to what impression your site makes and where you might need to focus more of your energy.

Scoring

If the responses to your five-second tests were overwhelmingly positive, you get 10 points. If there's no clear purpose expressed on the site, 0 points.

Improving Your Score: Creating an Effective Home Page

If your library home page didn't do so well with the five-second test, take heart: we've seen all sorts of libraries (from the tiny and underfunded to the large and affluent) make the mistake of putting too many options and too much content on their home pages out of pure altruism. Put another way: we have so much great stuff, we want everyone to know about it as soon as they get to our website! A noble goal, to be sure, but as your five-second test will attest, too much stuff on your home page obscures everything and showcases nothing. So here are a couple of strategies to create an effective home page for your library.

CRITICAL TASKS REVISITED Once again, thinking about your site's critical tasks will help you. Compare your current home page with the list of your site's critical tasks that you came up with in checkpoint 7.2. Your home page should make all of these things not just available, but easily available. So, for instance, there should be more than just a link to your catalog. There should be a prominently placed search box available for people to use.

BRAND BOLDLY When rethinking your home page, concentrate on your site's critical tasks, but don't forget about giving users a sense of what's going on in the library in general. You can do this by displaying your brand strongly (something Cambridge Libraries and Galleries, discussed above, certainly does well) and by highlighting your events prominently.

7.8 Website Is Easy to Use on All Devices

Why This Is Important   DIFFICULTY RATING: ★ ★ ★

Have you traveled by air recently? Electronic boarding passes, the myriad devices entertaining frustrated travelers, and onboard Wi-Fi are reminders of the web's ever-growing ubiquity and the diversity of the devices that connect us to it.

Like it or not, library websites are part of this evolution. Check your website analytics. We're sure that the amount of people accessing your site on mobile devices and tablets has increased in the past year. Designing our online services solely for people sitting at desks with a desktop computer is shortsighted.

Assessing Your Library

It won't be difficult for you to test your website on a few different devices. You won't even have to buy devices for testing. Remember, these devices are ubiquitous, so chances are that you'll be able to rustle some up from library staff. We suggest testing your site on iOS devices (iPhone, iPad) and a few devices running the Android operating system. The browsers on these devices usually do a fairly good job of scaling websites. Click around and explore your site. Can you easily accomplish critical tasks?

Scoring

This checkpoint is pretty much an all-or-nothing one. Special mobile site or responsive design? Score 10 points. Nothing of the sort? Give yourself 0 points.

Improving Your Score: Responsive Web Design (RWD)

While the browsers on mobile devices usually do a decent job of displaying websites, ideally your site will be designed in a way that works optimally on mobile browsers. An emerging best practice is using a technique called responsive web design (RWD).

With RWD, websites scale appropriately to any device, no matter the resolution of its display. This provides an optimized viewing experience and reduces the

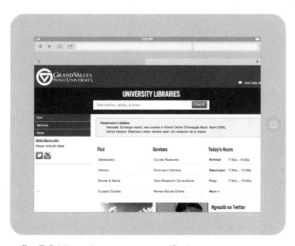

fig. 7.8 Library home page on an iPad.

fig. 7.9 Library home page on an iPhone.

amount of scrolling, swiping, pinching, and zooming often required when using websites on a mobile device. See figures 7.8 and 7.9 for an example of how a responsive website displays on different screen sizes.

We won't get into exploring the technical bits that make RWD work, but luckily there's a plethora of information about it on the web. Ethan Marcotte's "Responsive Web Design" (http://alistapart.com/articles/responsive-web-design), the first article to use the term, is a good starting point. See the "Additional Readings" section at the end of this chapter for more.

Responsive Problems

While it is easy enough to use responsive design for our websites, sadly, our control over the situation ends there. The things our websites connect people to—catalogs and research databases, for instance—aren't likely to display well on mobile devices. This is a problem. Aside from putting pressure on vendors to get with the program, there's no real practical option for improving the situation.

7.9 Website Employs the Library's Visual Language

Why This Is Important   DIFFICULTY RATING: ★ ★ ★

At the end of checkpoint 6.1, we encouraged you to list all of the places you'll employ the visual language described in your brand manual. We suggested that your website be one of those places, and this is a reminder.

It is important that all of your library's touchpoints have a similar look and feel. Having a unified design will help your library facilitate a consistent and cohesive user experience, increasing the amount of trust members have in your institution. And the more places you employ your library's visual language, the more effective it will be.

Your website is a highly trafficked touchpoint that can help you establish your library's brand. Make sure you take advantage of this by aligning the visual design of your website with the visual design of other library touchpoints. In practical terms, this means your website will use the same color palette, typefaces, and tone as your signs and brochures and other marketing materials.

Assessing Your Library

This one is easy to assess. Your website employs the library's visual language or it doesn't. And while this checkpoint is easy to assess, complying is a bit more involved. After all, you'll need to develop a visual language (see chapter 6, "Signage and Wayfinding") and then apply it to your website. But after you're done, your website will have the same look and feel as your print materials and signs.

Scoring

Here's another easy one to score. You get 5 points if your website has the same look and feel as your library's other products.

Improving Your Score: Implementing Your Library's Visual Language

To improve your score on this checkpoint, you'll most likely have to develop a visual language. You might also have to redesign your website. This will take a fair amount of time and effort, true. But it is absolutely necessary if you want to create an amazing user experience.

7.10 You Use Social Media Tools in Meaningful Ways

DIFFICULTY RATING: ★

It should come as no surprise to you that your web presence doesn't end with your library website. Your web presence includes all the other online tools you might use to reach out to, communicate with, and engage your members. This checkpoint is all about making sure you're doing all those things in a way that is meaningful to those members.

Why This Is Important

Social media is so amazingly pervasive that it's sometimes difficult to remember the social media landscape of five years ago. In those early days, libraries seemed to jump on the bandwagon eagerly, creating a presence on every social media platform available, on the off chance that some of their members might be in those spaces. Thankfully, we've reached a stage of maturity in social media, and we can be a bit more selective about where we choose to focus our efforts. Why? Because having a social media presence isn't about novelty anymore. It's about adding value.

Assessing and Scoring

In order to do an honest assessment of how meaningful your social media presence is, you would do no better than to take that question straight to your members. Try putting together a short survey listing your top three social media presences (you can assess "top three" any way you'd like; we suggest choosing the three social media accounts that you put the most time and effort into) and asking your members if they know about each presence. So, for example, your survey might look something like this:

1. Did you know the library is on
   a. Facebook? (Yes/No)
   b. Twitter? (Yes/No)
   c. Pinterest? (Yes/No)

Score 5 points if you get more "yes" replies than "no," 2 points if responses are split evenly, and 0 points if you get more "no" responses.

Improving Your Score: Getting to Meaningful Engagement on Social Media

There are all sorts of reasons why you might score poorly on this checkpoint. It could be that your members just didn't know about that Facebook page, or maybe your members aren't on Pinterest at all. Whatever the reason, the following should provide you with some ideas for how to engage more meaningfully with your community on social media.

PIMP YOUR PRESENCE Just as you would market any service the library provides, you should also market your social media presence. This could be as simple as adding links to your Facebook or Twitter (or whatever) accounts on printed materials like bookmarks or promoting those presences on your library's home page.

FOCUS YOUR ENERGIES Do a survey of your community to find out where they spend their time online. If you have a strong Twitter user community, then the library would obviously benefit from starting a Twitter account. If your members are more likely to be on Facebook, start a Facebook page for the library. The bottom line is you are more likely to see better, more meaningful engagement with members online if you are using the same tools they are.

UP THE ENGAGEMENT FACTOR Speaking of social media maturity, you've probably already figured out that using social media only for one-way communication from you to your members is shortsighted and does not really tap into the power of the platforms. So stop using your Twitter or Facebook account simply to broadcast your news feed and start using it to ask questions of your members, have conversations with them, respond to their information needs, and be a conduit for them to find and meaningfully engage with *each other*.

INVOLVE MEMBERS IN DEVELOPING YOUR SOCIAL MEDIA PRESENCE If you're having a difficult time getting to the level of engagement you'd like, you might try involving your members in *developing* your social media presence. For example, why not have community members tweet on behalf of the library? Or, if you're at an academic library, have your student advisory group manage your Facebook presence. Getting members involved in this way can up the level of community engagement in your social media efforts in remarkable ways.

7.11 Additional Reading

Don't Make Me Think, 2nd ed., by Steve Krug (New Riders, 2005), www.amazon
.com/dp/0321344758

Letting Go of the Words, 2nd ed., by Ginnie Reddish (Morgan Kaufmann, 2012),
www.amazon.com/dp/0123859301

Rocket Surgery Made Easy, by Steve Krug (New Riders, 2009), www.amazon.com/
dp/0321657292

"How We Do Usability Testing," by Matthew Reidsma, November 15, 2011, http://
matthew.reidsrow.com/articles/13

Center for Plain Language, http://centerforplainlanguage.org

"Guidelines for Visualizing Links," by Jakob Nielsen, May 10, 2004, www.nngroup
.com/articles/guidelines-for-visualizing-links

Chapter 8

Using the Library

▶ **MOST OF THIS BOOK HAS DEALT WITH SPECIFIC TYPES OF TOUCHPOINTS** that our members come into contact with when they use our resources and services—our signs, our policies, our service desks, our websites, and our physical spaces. But there is also a whole slew of additional touchpoints that members interact with in our buildings, like our public computers and technology infrastructure, our collections, and our events, among other things. This chapter tackles all those touchpoints and provides some ideas for how to improve our members' experiences using libraries and accomplishing tasks.

8.1 The Technology in Your Library Is Relevant, Useful, and Usable

DIFFICULTY RATING: ★ ★

Once upon a time, you could walk into a library, find things you want to read and use, and walk back out with a stack of materials to take home with you, all without ever having to interact with technology. While that might still be the case on the odd (very odd) occasion, you'd be hard-pressed to find a member in your building at any given time who hasn't interacted with a piece of technology since getting there, whether it be a public computer to search the catalog, your wireless network via her own web-enabled device, or any other of several technological devices in your building. Our lives are increasingly mediated by technology, so if your library isn't already thinking about how your members experience the technology in your buildings, now is the time to start.

Why This Is Important

Take a minute to think about all the technology you have in your building. Here's a list to get you started:

- public computers
- laptops
- tablets
- photocopiers/printers
- scanners
- VCRs
- DVD players
- televisions
- microform readers/printers
- automated check-in and check-out machines
- wireless Internet access
- e-book readers
- MP3 players
- digital cameras

That's already a lot of technology to consider, and it's only just a start; you probably have a lot more you could add to that list, especially if you loan an array of portable electronic devices to your members.

When you think about all those devices and interfaces en masse, you could easily get overwhelmed by the magnitude of the task ahead of you as you ask yourself how you could *possibly* ensure that *everything* is easy to use! Before you allow yourself to be burdened by the magnitude of that task though, we ask you to think about how your *members* feel about using all those devices and interfaces. Put yourself in their shoes for a moment and consider how challenging it may be for them to figure out how some of those things work, which is probably what they have to do every time they darken your doors. Once you've considered their perspective, you might find yourself feeling a tiny bit of surprise that people even come into your library anymore, given all the hoops you make them jump through to use your technology!

Assessing and Scoring

So let's talk about those hoops and try to assess them. As we mentioned previously, there's a lot to consider in this checkpoint, and we don't think there's an easy way to get an overall sense of how you're doing with technology in general or how your members feel about using the technology in your building. So we propose assessing a few discrete things.

First of all, let's take a look at your Wi-Fi. Is it easy to connect to? Here's a good test: if your website has a page that explains how to connect to your Wi-Fi, you're doing something wrong. Forget barcodes, forget passwords. The most you should make your members do is click on or touch one button. Ideally, they'd just have to select your network and they'd be connected. If your Wi-Fi is that easy to connect to, score 10 points. If it isn't, 0 points for you.

Secondly, let's talk about printing in your building. Is it easy for members to use your printers? Start by listing all of the steps it takes for a member to print a document. Do they have to buy credits on a special printing card and then visit a different computer to release the print job? That can make for a complicated process. Another good way to assess the level of difficulty here is to do a random count of how many questions you get at your service desks about printing. Keep track over the course of two weeks. If, after two weeks, less than 10 percent of your service desk questions are about printing, score 10 points. If it's more than 10 percent, score 0 points.

Finally, turn your attention to other self-service technology like scanners or self-check machines. Both types of devices can be tricky to use, so we're not going to assume that they are intuitive enough to not require help. But the question is, have you provided simple, easy-to-follow instructions for these devices? If your scanners/self-check machines have simple instructions that are easy to find, score five points. If they don't, score 0 points.

There is a maximum of 25 points for this checkpoint. Add up your score and record it in the appendix.

Improving Your Score: Doing Technology Better

A few paragraphs ago, we admitted that technology is a huge consideration for any library and that because there are so many varied tech-related things in our buildings, there's no *easy* way to make life simpler and better for our members. While we stand by that statement, we also believe that there are a lot of little improvements we can make to our tech environments that can improve our members' experience in our buildings. Here's a list of those improvements.

YOUR COMPUTING ENVIRONMENT SUPPORTS WHAT MEMBERS USE AND PREFER
There are two predominant operating systems out there—Windows and OS X. Is
your library an all-Windows or all-OS X environment? Either scenario is equally
problematic. Forcing your members to use an operating system that they are unfa-
miliar with makes their experience at your library uncomfortable at best and frustrating at worst. Providing access to both operating systems and allowing members
to choose which they would prefer to use shows sensitivity to their needs and preferences.

YOUR COMPUTING ENVIRONMENT IS NOT UNDULY RESTRICTIVE We understand
that managing a fleet of public access computers is a massive undertaking. There
are so many things that people can do on those computers, from downloading
unwanted software to unsuspectingly introducing malware/viruses to the network,
that it can be a challenge for any IT department. We get that public access computers can be a huge nightmare to administer. Having said that, what we'd really like
to caution against is the temptation to lock down your computers to such an extent
that your members can't do what they need to on them. It's a fine line, and every
library will have to figure out for itself where it is comfortable drawing that line. We
just feel the need to issue a reminder that sometimes the "ounce of prevention is
worth a pound of cure" mindset might make things so restrictive for your members
that the frustration on their part outweighs any peace of mind gained by IT.

PUBLIC PRINTING/COPYING IS EASY While we'd love to suggest that we all aban-
don any/all chargeback mechanisms for public printing/copying in the interest of
improving the user experience at our libraries, we fully sympathize with the reality
of shrinking library budgets. Most of us simply can't get rid of the fee hoop here,
and that's okay. But there are other hoops we can remove—for example, by providing free printing/copying for small jobs that max out at five pages. If you've ever
worked at a public service desk and dealt with a rushed member who needs to print
just a page or two and is frustrated by having to purchase a printing card to do so,
you can probably see the value in such a policy. Another service offering to consider
is wireless printing. As your library statistics surely demonstrate, more and more
people bring their own devices into the library, so having a mechanism for members to print from their own devices is a no-brainer.

EASY WI-FI In the preceding "Assessing and Scoring" section, we handed out 10
points to every library that has an open Wi-Fi network that doesn't require mem-

bers to type in a password or a barcode. Conversely, we gave 0 points to those libraries that do require members to log in to the wireless network. The moral of the story? Not having to log in to a Wi-Fi network is just easier for your members, period. Of course, depending on the type of library you work in, an open Wi-Fi network may not be an option. All we ask is that you take a good, hard look at why you require members to log in to your Wi-Fi network and seriously consider changing that requirement if you have any flexibility to do so.

SELF-SERVE DEVICES ARE INTUITIVE AND/OR HAVE EASY-TO-FOLLOW INSTRUCTIONS
Do your scanners, microform readers/printers, self-check machines, photocopiers, printers, and any other self-serve devices include easy-to-find and easy-to-follow instructions on how to use them? If they don't, get to work creating some. When you have no control over how intuitive a piece of equipment is (and most of us don't when it comes to things like scanners, printers, etc.), the least you can do to make your members' lives easier is to provide clear, simple instructions for how to use that equipment.

GET MEMBERS INVOLVED IN EQUIPMENT ACQUISITIONS If you have a library advisory group, why not enlist their help when it comes time to acquire new equipment? Whether it's new public access computers, scanners, self-check machines, or loanable devices like laptops, tablets, or e-book readers, it's your members who will be the ones using the equipment, so why not allow them to have a say in what's purchased?

8.2 Collections Are Relevant to Member Needs

DIFFICULTY RATING: ★ ★

The title of this checkpoint reads a bit like what should be the number one universal principle for libraries: we should have stuff in our collections that our members want to read, watch, listen to, or use in some way. The end. No more need be said about that.

But wait! This isn't a remedial lesson in Creating a Library 101; it's about why we need to think about being responsive to member needs in how we build our collections. And it's about some of the ways we can actually do that. Unless you work in a library where 100 percent of your collection circulates on a regular basis, you probably want to keep reading.

Why This Is Important

A vegetarian walks into a new restaurant on her block and takes a look at the menu. Seeing no vegetarian options, except for an uninspired salad, our vegetarian walks back out again and heads for her favorite lunch counter, where she knows she will have many options from which to choose. Does she return to the new restaurant the next day? Definitely not. The following week? No. The following year? Unlikely. Why? Because she's seen what they have to offer and she can't eat any of it.

You can see where we're going with that thinly veiled allegory. If your library collections do not meet the needs of your community, whatever those needs are, your community will not use your library. Period. That is a universal principle that we all know to be true. However, it's not quite that simple, is it? Because while you may serve a single "community," its needs are probably extremely diverse, so you're probably serving some of those needs, but maybe not most. We think you can probably do better, but before exploring how, let's assess where you're at first.

Assessing and Scoring

To determine how well your collections meet the needs of your members, we recommend doing a couple of things: a survey and a focus group. For the survey, target every person who checks out an item from the library during a specific period of time (a week or two should do it). Either hand surveys to members at the circulation desk or include a URL to an online survey on their checkout slips (particularly handy if you use self-check machines). On your survey, ask two questions:

1. Name one item you checked out today.
2. Is the item you named
   a. exactly what you came in for?
   b. not what you came in for but on the same topic?
   c. not related to what you came in for at all?

As you can see, this survey doesn't get into the "whys" at all (Why isn't what you checked out exactly what you came in for? Why are you leaving with something entirely unrelated to what you wanted in the first place? Etc.). But it will give you a snapshot of how your collection fares in meeting your members' needs (in an admittedly unscientific way).

Score 8 points if more than half your survey respondents chose 2(a), 4 points if more than half your survey respondents chose 2(b), and 0 points if more than half chose 2(c).

For the focus group, gather five to seven library members and have a conversation about how well the library collections meet their needs. Ask questions about what they usually use the library for and if they usually find things in the library that they borrow. Be careful to steer the conversation away from how easy or difficult it is to *find* materials, either in the catalog or in the building, and keep things at a more general level. You'll have to be your own judge when it comes to scoring your focus group results. Give yourself 7 points if the results are overwhelmingly positive, 3 points if they were more positive than negative, and 0 points if you heard more negative comments than positive ones.

Add your focus group score to your survey score and record your total (max 15 points) in the appendix.

Improving Your Score: Member-Driven Collection Building
If we were to guess at the results for this checkpoint, we'd say that most libraries score in around the middle range, where there's evidence that some needs are being met but there's still room for improvement. Check out these ideas for ways to be more member-driven in how you build your collections.

LEARN ABOUT YOUR COMMUNITY You might already have demographic information about your community, which is great. But demographics can only get you so far when it comes to building collections your community might need and use. Take your research a step further by going back to chapter 2, where we discuss user research methodologies, and tap into some of those methodologies to learn more about your community. We recommend interviews and cultural probes. Getting to the heart of user goals and motivations will give you a lot of great evidence to work with when it comes to buying materials for your library.

BUILD PERSONAS Use the results from your user interviews and cultural probes exercises to build three to five personas for your library. As we mention many times in this book, personas can help you in all aspects of design in your library, including building collections. Go back to chapter 2, section 2.2, for more on personas.

TALK TO NON-MEMBERS There could be any number of reasons why members of your community don't use your library, just one of which might be that your collections are irrelevant to their needs. Get out into your community and try to learn about those people who never visit the library, either physically or virtually. Sometimes just being an active member of your own community could mean that you meet a few of these folks, so try and learn about them if you do meet them. Or take a more calculated approach to finding out about non-members by setting up a table at your community center or mall and inviting people to fill in a survey or just come talk to you. You will probably learn way more about them than just what their collections needs are, and that's a good thing.

BUILD YOUR COLLECTIONS WITH MEMBERS IN MIND   One of the most common buzz phrases you will hear in the collections business these days is "Patron-Driven Acquisition" (PDA). PDA moves collection building away from the historical notion that libraries should build a balanced collection that stands the test of time, and toward the idea that collections need to serve the purposes of the library's members today. Probably the best way to introduce PDA into your collection environment is to set aside a portion of your materials budget for PDA, allow users to select materials they want/need, and use that PDA budget to fill those requests. PDA can work for physical and electronic items, and many vendors provide models for ways to include PDA in your collections workflow. If you're keen to explore this option, there's all manner of library collection development literature devoted to the topic that you'd benefit from reading. See the "Additional Reading" section of this chapter for some suggestions.

USE YOUR INTERLIBRARY LOAN DATA   If your library offers interlibrary loan services, a surefire way to explore what members want that you don't have is to pore over those ILL requests. Look for patterns that identify holes in your collection and fill those holes by buying titles on those topics.

USE YOUR E-RESOURCE DATA   Having collections that are relevant to member needs isn't just about buying new stuff; it's also about retaining stuff that people use. So look at your e-resource usage data. Is no one using that expensive database? Promote it for a few weeks, then monitor usage. If it stays low or drops any further, cancel that subscription and divert those precious funds elsewhere.

8.3 Marketing Materials Are Relevant to Member Needs

DIFFICULTY RATING: ★ ★

Do the booklists, bookmarks, brochures, and newsletters you create do nothing more than pile up around the library, making it look like a cluttered mess? Have you recently found a "readalikes" list for a book that was popular four years ago? Is that "How to Search Our Databases" trifold not flying from its plastic stand? Maybe it's time to assess how well the marketing materials you create for your members actually meet their needs.

This checkpoint isn't about the visual design of your marketing materials; chapter 6 deals with that issue. Nor is this checkpoint about how to declutter your spaces; checkpoint 3.2 can help you there. What this checkpoint does is provide some ways to test the usefulness of your marketing materials to your members while offering some advice on how to do better.

Why This Is Important

If you've ever spent time in a waiting room and looked around for something to read, only to find well-thumbed magazines from a decade ago, you know what a turnoff it can be when you're surrounded by dusty reading materials that are irrelevant to you. That's a tiny indication of how your members feel when they walk into your library, head for the information stand, and twirl it around, only to be faced with supposedly "helpful" materials that are outdated, unattractive, and don't address a single one of their needs.

As a helping profession, we tend to create these things on the fly, ostensibly to help certain members and address needs as they come up. What we should be doing, instead, is taking a planned, thoughtful approach to developing promotional and marketing materials that actually meet member needs.

Assessing and Scoring

You might be faced with a situation where you're trying to pare back a collection of marketing materials that you've inherited from former staff members. Or maybe you've recently been put in charge of managing such a collection, but the content of each promotional piece actually "belongs" to a specific department or staff member. How do you go about wrangling such a collection?

Much like we suggested in checkpoint 6.2 ("All signage uses the same visual language"), it is a good idea to conduct an audit of your library's print promotional materials. Knowing exactly what the library is producing, where it lives, and who is responsible for it will help you keep track of what's being produced and whether it is compliant with this checkpoint.

We suggest creating a spreadsheet with six columns to track the following information:

- Location(s)
- Material type (bookmark, brochure, handout, newsletter, poster, etc.)
- Last updated (date)
- Employs visual language? (Yes/No)
- Appropriately written? (Yes/No)
- Still relevant? (Yes/No)

The first three columns will be easy to complete. The next two (visual language and appropriately written) will require a bit of an assessment on your part, so take some time to complete those.

To complete the last column (relevance), we recommend a simple participatory exercise that you can take to your members at large. Clear off a large bulletin board in a public area and pin up all your print marketing materials to the board. Beside each, pin up a blank sheet of paper. At the top of the board, ask a simple question: "Do you use these materials?" Don't ask if people *like* them or think they're *useful*, ask specifically if they *use* them. What you really want to gauge with this exercise is not if your members think your print materials are nice, or if they think they are useful, but whether or not they *actually use them*. Keep a marker handy and ask members to place a checkmark on the blank piece of paper beside each handout they actually use. Keep your display up for a couple of weeks (any longer and folks will start to get used to it and, therefore, ignore it), and at the end of the two-week period, you should have a pretty decent indication of the usefulness of each of your print marketing materials.

Add this information to the "still relevant" column on your spreadsheet. Once you're done with your audit and assessment, don't delete the spreadsheet—instead, use it as on ongoing audit, keeping track of any new print products.

To score your library on this checkpoint, give yourself 10 points if more than 50 percent of your print materials scored well with members, 5 points if less than 50 percent scored well, and 0 points if less than 25 percent of your materials scored well.

Improving Your Score: Creating and Sustaining a Useful, Relevant Collection of Print Marketing Materials

If you completed the audit and member exercise we outlined above, good for you. You're already well on your way to a more useful, relevant collection of print marketing materials. Here are a few more ideas for how to get there.

TRACK TRENDS AT SERVICE DESKS Have regular meetings with your public service staff (monthly should do it) to find out what the number one question asked by members is every month. In some months, you might want to create a print aid to address the question right away; at other times, you might want to see if a question trends for a few months before creating something to address it. You will want to use your own discretion on how often to create print materials to address common questions, but most important, make sure you're using evidence to guide you in what materials to create in the first place.

CONSIDER ONLINE ALTERNATIVES We all have legacy handouts lying around our libraries. Hopefully your audit uncovered those items and you're already doing something about them. One legacy that you might still be living with is a collection of print handouts that were useful in print a while ago, but that might make more sense now as an online learning object. Handouts on how to search databases or find articles come to mind here. When databases first started showing up at libraries on tapes and CD-ROMs, it made sense to offer handouts on how to search a particular database when members sat down at a terminal to use it. Nowadays, we're hard pressed to find a database that isn't online, and print "how to" guides simply don't make much sense for online databases. So why not consider converting that guide to an online video or screencast instead?

ONGOING MEMBER INVOLVEMENT The best way to ensure a sustained, evidence-based approach to print marketing materials is to keep asking for your members' opinions. When you have an idea for something new, why not take that idea to your members (via whatever channels you have available to you) to seek their input on the utility of the proposed new piece? Remember that if you ask for opinions alone ("What do you think?"), that is all you'll get (and people tend to err on the side of politeness when asked for opinions), so be sure to ask about utility and usefulness instead.

USE YOUR PERSONAS In chapter 2, section 2.2, we talked about how creating personas for your library can help you target your resources and services to the people you actually serve. If you've already created your personas, go back to them every time you come up with an idea for a new piece of print marketing and ask yourself if any of them would actually find it useful. And if you haven't created your personas yet, what are you waiting for?

8.4 You Merchandize Your Materials

DIFFICULTY RATING: ★

If you've walked into any bricks-and-mortar retail establishment in the last ten years, you know that merchandizing products is the name of the retail game. There are studies after studies devoted to consumer behavior in retail environments, all manner of research into the placement of products on shelves, and whole marketing books devoted to the topic of merchandizing. This checkpoint is not going to reproduce all of that wisdom. But we will talk about why merchandizing matters in libraries and how we can learn a few lessons from retail environments.

Why This Is Important

As simple as it is to merchandize your materials, we've seen plenty of libraries—mostly academic libraries but some public libraries, too—that don't bother. This is a real shame because merchandizing is an extremely effective way to connect people with content they might not even be looking for. These sorts of serendipitous discoveries make libraries exciting and bring our collections to life. In fact, this physical discovery process scratches an itch that online experiences often don't, so we should almost think of it as a competitive advantage over those ubiquitous and easy online book-shopping experiences. There's interesting content hiding in the stacks of your library. Why not give it a place to shine?

Merchandizing is all about improving the visibility of your collections. You might imagine that a well-merchandized library collection looks similar to a well-merchandized bookstore—tables in visible areas with new, high-use, or themed titles; shelf endcaps with select materials on display; select titles in regular stacks shelved with their covers facing out. These are just some of the merchandizing ideas you see in an average bookstore, ideas that we've also seen in some well-merchandized libraries.

Assessing and Scoring

Assessing and scoring how well your library does on this checkpoint is fairly easy—either you're displaying materials on tables and endcaps or you're not. If you are, score 20 points.

Of course, merchandizing alone isn't enough. You will also want to assess whether or not materials from your displays are getting checked out. If they aren't, you might want to reconsider your displays and the materials you are highlighting.

Improving Your Score: Highlighting Your Collections

Whether your library is new to collection merchandizing or not, here are a few ideas for ways to better draw attention to your collections.

DON'T DITCH THE DUST JACKET Many libraries get shelf-ready materials from vendors that come preprocessed, stamped, labeled, and ready for members to borrow. This lovely service saves us all sorts of time but can sometimes leave our books looking less than inviting, especially when part of the processing includes getting rid of dust jackets for hardcover books. Thankfully, more and more book-processing vendors are making this practice optional, so if you have the choice of retaining or recycling your dust jackets, opt for the former. As you're probably well aware, most hardcover books without dust jackets aren't worth merchandizing at all.

THEMATIC DISPLAYS Having a table of new/hot materials is a no-brainer, but you might also want to consider frequently changing displays of collections that are based around timely or local themes. We've seen thematic displays around everything from a local election to global news, pop culture events like movie openings, and national sporting events. The options really are limited only by your imagination!

IMPULSE CHECKOUTS Ever wondered why grocery stores place confections and tabloid magazines right beside checkouts? Because people are more likely to pick up a candy bar or a magazine that claims to uncover everything that's wrong with the Kardashians while they wait in line to pay for their groceries than they would if they saw those same items as they strolled down the regular aisles. They're called impulse purchases for a reason! If you merchandized materials at your self-check machines or circulation desk, you'd probably see a similar uptake in impulse checkouts (minus the empty calories and celebrity gossip).

RECENT RETURNS Many online retailers draw attention to other shoppers' habits in order to coax us to behave the same way. That's why you often see "people who bought this also bought X" displays on e-commerce interfaces. Why? Because there's something in human psychology that makes us want to know what other people like us are doing. Tapping into that notion, we've seen some libraries prominently display recently returned items under the assumption that other members might be interested in what fellow borrowers have been reading/watching/listening to. If you can pull circulation data out of your system, you might even be able to provide compelling visualizations of that data on a digital display in your library. An interesting example is the Awesome Box from the Harvard Library Innovation Lab. When a library member places an item into an Awesome Box, not only is the item prominently displayed, a Tweet is sent out and the item is included on an online list of the "Recently Awesome" (http://librarylab.law.harvard.edu/awesome).

8.5 Library Services and Programs Solve Problems

Why This Is Important   DIFFICULTY RATING: ★ ★ ★

Library services are the very reason libraries—and all of the library touchpoints we've been thinking about in this book—exist. Without library services, there are no libraries. Because they are so essential, it makes sense that libraries need to be mindful of how library services impact the experiences they provide.

In the introduction to this book, we stated that libraries should strive to be *useful*, *usable* and *desirable*. We like those concepts so much that we included them in the title of this book. Much of what we've talked about has been devoted to improving the usability and desirability of libraries. Making these improvements will definitely improve your members' experience, but you can't stop there. In checkpoint 7.4, we pointed out that no amount of amazing visual design can make people use a library website that is filled with unappealing content. The same principle applies to our libraries as a whole. A library can have an amazing building filled with friendly librarians and top-notch signage, but if its services are irrelevant, no one will use it.

This checkpoint comes last not because we've been ignoring it throughout this book, and not because we want you to do everything else in this book before thinking about this checkpoint. We've saved it for last because, in many ways, it is *the most important checkpoint*. It will challenge you to rethink your services and explore new opportunities.

What Is a Problem?

It's worth taking a moment to talk about the word *problem*. In one sense of the word, a problem is a puzzle that needs to be solved. Take math problems—they are simply puzzles in search of solutions. But the notion of *problem as puzzle* can be used to describe more than just equations. We can also use it as a way to analyze someone's behavior. Here's an example: Hannah is ordering tea at a café. Why? There could be a number of reasons:

- She's thirsty and finds tea refreshing.
- She enjoys the taste of tea.
- She needs to order a drink to use the Wi-Fi.

The simple act of ordering tea can be the result of very different motivations. Like this example of ordering tea, using the word *problem* in the sense of *a puzzle to be solved* unravels a way for us to think about what people need, and how libraries can respond.

A more literal—and commonly used—sense of the word *problem* refers to a distressing issue, or something that needs to be fixed. For instance, the problem of global warming or homelessness. There's not much more to explain about this sense of the word since we use it all the time.

When we say that library services should solve problems, we mean it in both of the senses we just discussed:

- Libraries will provide better services if they think about member needs as problems to be solved.
- Libraries should help solve real problems in their communities.

Assessing and Scoring

As you might imagine, this is not a simple checkpoint to score. But we think it's important enough that you should put as much time and effort as you need to in order to assess your current situation. To do so, we recommend using two user research techniques in particular: interviews and cultural probes.

USER INTERVIEWS Talk to five to seven community members. Try not to recruit existing library members only; include a few non-members as well. Ask open-ended questions about their lives, their needs, their goals, and their motivations. Don't even ask about the library if you can avoid it because talking about the library will put a focus or a particular lens on what they tell you. Keep the conversation broad and general. The goal for these interviews is to end up with snapshots of community members' lives so you can think about when and where the library can become problem solvers in those lives.

CULTURAL PROBES Recruit another five to seven community members (again, don't limit yourself to just library members). Provide each recruit with a point-and-shoot still camera and a blank journal. Ask them to take pictures and use their journals to tell their own stories. Run the exercise for at least a few weeks so you have lots of data at the end. Give your subjects guidelines on their output (e.g., take at least one picture a day and write at least one journal entry every two days) and prompts for what to include. Just as with the interviews, the goal of this exercise is to end up with snapshots of the lives of five to seven community members.

HOW DO YOU SCORE? There's no simple rubric for scoring a library on how well its services and programs solve the community's problems. After doing the two research explorations outlined above, you will have a better sense of the unique problems of your community, so that's a start. For the purposes of this exercise, give yourself 30 points if you feel that your library is already doing a good job of solving those problems with your existing services and programs; 15 points if you think you're doing an adequate job; and 0 points if you see lots of room for improvement.

Improving Your Score: Improving Services by Solving Problems

If you scored in the bottom half of the simple assessment above, don't despair. We've got a number of ideas to share regarding how to improve your services to a point where you're actively solving problems in your community. First, let's talk some more about how to get there.

Conceptualizing our services as solutions to members' problems puts us in a user-centered frame of mind. Not only is it a point of view focused on helping, it also enables us to examine people's goals and root motivations. When we know more about those, we can create interesting solutions to meet their needs and make deep connections.

Let's think about a common library act—using a computer to access the web. What's the problem being solved by the library? On one level, the problem is obvious: *I want to access the web.*

But what's really going on with our web-browsing member? Is she looking for work because she's out of a job? Is she entertaining herself on YouTube because she's bored? Is she trying to finish writing a paper? Is she attempting to learn about her favorite hobby to improve her skills? Her objective might be to access the web, but her motivation probably runs a lot deeper.

Let's pretend she wants to learn about her favorite hobby to improve her skills. Now let's take it a step further. Why does she want to improve her skills? What problem is that solving? Perhaps she's competitive and wants to be better than her friend. Perhaps she wants to learn more so she can teach others.

We could give the same sort of scrutiny to all other library services: people using library materials, attending programs, using our spaces, and more. And we *should* put people under the microscope to figure out their motivations. The deeper we dive into our members' lives, the greater the impact we can have on those lives. The greater impact we have, the more we'll be valued. Creating services that are truly valuable is the best form of library advocacy. It is the key to becoming essential to our communities.

So instead of thinking only about how your library can provide programs and services that your members might want, need, and use, start thinking about how your programs and services can be solutions to your members' problems. Remember, people don't come to the library to read books or use your Wi-Fi. They come to the library to learn, improve, be entertained, and connect, and reading books and going online are just two ways to help them get there. Designing services to help people do these things will help your library evolve beyond being a warehouse for content.

Tip

Thinking of our libraries in terms of problems to be solved is also quite useful for marketing efforts. A marketing campaign based on member behavior might say, "Come to the library to check out books." A campaign based on problem solving might instead proclaim, "The library will make your life better!" Clearly, the latter has the potential to make a bigger impression *and* have more of an impact.

Libraries Solving Community Problems

This isn't a radical idea. Until not so very long ago, information was a scarce resource, and libraries solved the very big problem of providing access to that resource—first by providing access to print materials, then by providing access to the web. Of course, once information became less scarce, as access to the web grew increasingly ubiquitous, the library's central role in being a problem solver in its community by providing access to information began to change. Except, many libraries held on to the notion that the singular value they offered to their community was in providing access to content, whether that content was commercial, professional, or scholarly.

Don't get us wrong: we like content. We certainly think there is still a role for libraries in being content purveyors. But we also think libraries can do a lot more to augment their role as information providers to better meet the needs of their communities and help solve problems. The very best examples of this sort of augmentation that we've seen are the result of libraries either partnering with other community organizations or expanding their own mandates to become integral to their communities. Here are a few of our favorite examples.

BALTIMARKET Baltimarket is a collaboration between the Enoch Pratt Free Library, the city of Baltimore, and other organizations to bring healthy food to food deserts (i.e., places where healthy, affordable food is difficult to obtain). People can order groceries online and pick them up at their local library branch. (See http://baltimore health.org/virtualsupermarket.html.)

ON-STAFF PUBLIC HEALTH NURSE Every public library collection contains health and wellness books, right? The Pima County (AZ) Public Library has taken its role of providing this type of info to the next level by having a public health nurse on staff at the library. The nurse leads programs and is available to answer questions, making referrals when appropriate. Combine this with expert help searching databases, and the potential to assist members with health and wellness issues is nearly endless. (See www.library.pima.gov/about.)

LIBRARYYOU LibraryYOU, a project from the Escondido (CA) Public Library, takes a new view of the library collection. It helps its community create and publish videos and podcasts "to collect and share local knowledge" (http://libraryyou.escondido.org).

STAFF SOCIAL WORKER When your library is located in a large, urban area, your locations can often become community hubs by virtue of their geography. Not surprisingly, urban library locations often have to contend with unique community issues like homelessness, substance abuse, and various forms of marginalization. Some libraries, like the San Francisco Public Library, have responded by hiring a social worker for their urban locations to assist members with their unique problems. (See "San Francisco Public Library Hires Social Worker to Help with

Homeless," *Library Journal*, January 11, 2010, www.libraryjournal.com/article/
CA6714375.html.)

Some might object to libraries getting involved with projects like these, claiming
that to do so is a sign of mission creep. We tend to think that such a narrow view
of the purpose of libraries is shortsighted. As people use increasingly varied means
of accessing content, it is more important than ever that libraries find new ways
to help their communities. Simply put, if you want your community to truly value
your library, your library must meet a need that no other organization can.

8.6 Additional Reading

"What Patron-Driven Acquisition (PDA) Does and Doesn't Mean: An FAQ," by
Rick Anderson, May 31, 2011, http://scholarlykitchen.sspnet.org/2011/
05/31/what-patron-driven-acquisition-pda-does-and-doesnt-mean-an-faq

Community-Led Libraries Toolkit, by the Working Together Project (Canada), www
.librariesincommunities.ca/resources/Community-Led_Libraries_Toolkit.pdf

Chapter 9

Wrapping Up: Philosophy, Process, and Culture

▶ **WE'VE HAD A LOT TO SAY ABOUT MANY DIFFERENT ASPECTS OF LIBRARIES** in the pages you've just read, so we're hoping you're already well armed with a whole slew of practical techniques and ideas for user-centered changes you can make at your library. In this final chapter, we delve into some context around how to make those changes: how to think holistically about the touchpoints at your library; a design process that you might find useful when tackling design challenges; the organizational culture necessary to be a truly user-centered library; and some final parting words to help you on your way.

9.1 Whole Library Thinking

If you've evaluated all of the checkpoints in this book, you know which of your library's touchpoints are facilitating a good user experience and which touchpoints need to be improved. You probably feel like digging in and improving the low-hanging fruit immediately. Good! We're not going to discourage that.

But library touchpoints don't exist in a vacuum. So before you start improving touchpoints in isolation, let's once again consider the needs of library members.

Even though you've analyzed and assessed touchpoints in discrete units, library members hardly ever use only one type of touchpoint to complete a library task.

Because your goal is to assess and improve people's *overall experiences*, it is very important that you consider the big picture and integrate touchpoints into a real-world context.

You can do this by thinking about what people are trying to do in your library. Remember the discussion of the critical tasks on your library website at checkpoint 7.2? This is similar. Ask yourself, "What are the most common things people want to accomplish by using our library?"

Here's a list of sample library tasks to help you get started making your own:

- Pick up a held item
- Print an essay before class
- Use a group study space
- Attend a library event
- Put a book on reserve for a class

Journey Maps

To think holistically about these critical library tasks, map out the steps a library member takes to complete them. Here's an example:

Picking Up a Held Item
- Place hold on library website (online presence)
- Receive notification email (online presence)
- Travel to library
- Park in lot (library building)
- Enter building (library building)
- Be greeted by librarian (customer service)
- Find holds location (signage)
- Walk to holds shelf (library building)
- Locate item (library furniture)
- Walk to circulation desk (library building)
- Interact with library worker (customer service)
- Exit building (library building)

This list tells us which types of touchpoints are used the most and illustrates how the touchpoints are connected.

Most important, lists like this can be used to assess the overall experience of completing a task. If the task is composed of touchpoints that need to be improved, library members probably aren't having a fun time completing the task. If the task has only one minor difficulty, or pain point, members are probably having a decent experience.

Creating journey maps for your library's common tasks can help you prioritize your improvement efforts. Compare the maps of your common tasks after creating them. Do any contain more pain points and areas of friction than others? Improve these first. Do any contain only minor pain points? Let these slide until you fix the big things. Remember, all of these touchpoints are used in library tasks that a lot of people do. Improving them will have a big impact.

Journey Maps for Innovating

Your journey maps can do more than help you remove pain points. They can also help you completely reenvision your services.

Asking the right questions can help expose more possibilities. For each touchpoint in a journey, list the following things:

- Assumptions about members at this touchpoint. What are their goals? What are they trying to accomplish?
- Assumptions about the touchpoint itself. Why is it the way it is?
- The goal of this touchpoint. Can it be accomplished in another way?
- Why is this touchpoint necessary? Can this journey be simpler or more engaging by removing this touchpoint? What could replace it?
- How does this touchpoint relate to the previous and next? What's the flow?

You can take this deep thinking a step further by rephrasing your list of critical library tasks. Notice that our list of sample library tasks at the beginning of this section is actually quite library-centered. It lists people's behavior *only in relation to the library* without exploring what people are actually trying to accomplish. Here are the tasks rewritten to reflect a broader perspective:

- Read a specific item outside of the library
- Get a good grade

Tip

You can take your journey map a step further and create an illustrated depiction of how the touchpoints are used and connected by plotting them on a map or floor plan. This will give you a concrete visualization that might spark more solutions for ways to streamline the entire experience. If you want to keep it simple and skip the illustration, go ahead. A simple list like the one in this section can be very effective, too.

- Read or study in a quiet space
- Be entertained or learn something in a group setting
- Get access to a specific book

Reconceptualizing library tasks like this will allow you to explore different ways to help people accomplish their goals. So for the first item, instead of concentrating on the item reservation and pick-up process, you might brainstorm and discuss things like home delivery and item kiosks in the community.

Discussing motivations behind library tasks and brainstorming responses with your team in a classic "no wrong answers" brainstorming session can generate new ideas and be a great catalyst for change. Test and implement the most promising ideas using the design process described in the next section.

9.2 The Design Process

Designing Your Library

Like we said in the introduction to this book, you're a designer whether you know it or not. Every time you make a decision about how something in your library looks or functions, you're making a design decision. See, we have a pretty loose definition of design: arranging elements for a particular purpose. While this might seem like a really broad definition, read on and it will make sense.

One of our goals with this book is to help librarians be intentional about design decisions and stop the plague of designing with defaults. Whether it's a default typeface, a default arrangement of furniture, or a default way of thinking—for instance, not taking a step back to see the bigger picture and continuing to do something the way it has always been done—default design decisions never yield results that will be optimal for your members.

Reading this book is a good first step toward designing with intention. We've considered how different parts of the library impact people's experiences, explored optimizing touchpoints, and discussed some big picture library thinking. You'll make better decisions after having read this book, but that is only the beginning. You can make even better decisions thinking of design not as a singular act but as a continual process.

The Design Process

There is a number of different design methodologies, but they share some common elements. Boiled down, they have four main components: observing, prototyping, testing, and implementing.

OBSERVING In this step, your goal is to learn about the problem you're trying to solve. The learning starts when you attempt to clearly state the problem. Example draft problem statements could include the following:

- Checkout lines are too long.
- Program attendance is low.
- Reference staff is too busy to answer all of the questions received.

Spend some time refining the statement. As usual, it helps to focus on library members. Here are two different ways to refine the first problem above:

- Members feel impatient waiting in line to check out items.
- The average checkout line wait time in the evening makes taking home items inconvenient.

The way the problem is phrased will impact the type of solution you create. The first statement might lead us toward a solution that deals with entertaining library members as they wait in line. The second statement might lead up to a solution that involves hiring more staff or installing self-check machines. These are two very different solutions to the original "Checkout lines are too long" statement. It's possible to come to faulty conclusions when refining your problem. If this happens, you'll be trying to solve the wrong problem, so making sure you're asking the right question is an important part of this step.

Once you know what problem you're trying to solve, you'll have to ask a lot of questions and dive deeply into each element of the situation. The "Journey Maps for Innovating" portion of the previous section is a good start for exploring all of the issues surrounding a particular service. You'll probably also want to employ a variety of user research techniques to learn more about the issue. Good tools for this include contextual inquiries and user interviews.

PROTOTYPING In this step, you'll think of potential solutions to the problem you're solving. To help generate ideas, break down the problem into discrete steps. Let's use Hannah, our tea drinker from checkpoint 8.5 ("Library services and programs solve problems"), as an example here. Remember, she wants to drink some tea but doesn't have any.

If there were a cup of tea in front of her, her problem would be easy to solve: she would pick up the tea and drink it. But since there's no tea prepared, solving the problem is more complicated. Here are a few possible solutions:

- Prepare some tea.
- Go to the café for tea.
- Ask my friend to deliver a cup of tea.

Each of these solutions contains its own set of mini-problems. To prepare tea, you need

- a mug
- hot water
- a tea bag

Like the initial problem—wanting tea—these three needs are problems that can all be solved in different ways.

I need a mug.
- Get one from the cabinet.
- Can I actually just use this glass on the counter?

I need hot water.
- Make some with the kettle.
- Use the instant hot water at the sink.

I need a tea bag.
- Get one from the cabinet.
- Should I use this loose-leaf tea and my infuser?

Thinking about the process of having a tea to drink in these discrete steps makes it seem impressive that any of us ever get anything accomplished! Truth be told, we solve problems like these for ourselves day in, day out, without any conscious thought. But taking the time to think about behavior in this way yields some interesting results. If we were in the business of selling tea, we'd want to examine all of the above problems to find opportunities for improving someone's tea-making experience. We're not, but we can still use this type of thinking to provide better library experiences. Breaking down people's library behaviors into such granular detail will give you the complete picture. Such detail might seem superfluous, but it isn't. It will help you overcome assumptions and can lead to some real innovations.

A good way to create prototypes is to start with a group brainstorming session. You know, the classic one in which there's no bad idea.

The group should list all sorts of solutions, and the group should talk them through. The sky is the limit for generating ideas, and oddball or unrealistic ideas should be actively encouraged. Not only are they a great way to get the group thinking in a different way, they can also be used to help explain what's good about other ideas. If appropriate, the best ideas should be combined and the group should agree on which ideas are worth pursuing. Once the group agrees upon some potential solutions, you'll need to see if your hunches are right by testing them.

Tip

By the way, if the line between prototyping solutions and observing the problem seems a bit blurred, you're on the right track. The four steps we've outlined aren't 100 percent linear. As you develop prototypes, you'll probably come to understand more about the problem. And that's a good thing! Use this to further refine what you're working on.

TESTING To test your prototypes you'll have to somehow expose them to library members and assess how the prototypes perform. For instance, if you're testing a new way to merchandise materials, you'd schedule time to create the display and track the rate of circulation. If you're testing a new navigational scheme for your website, you'd conduct some usability tests.

By testing your prototypes you'll know if you're on the right track to finding your solution. If your prototype doesn't live up to your solution, don't worry! Think of this prototyping and testing process as a way to fail often, and fail fast. It is much better to find out what works and what doesn't work in a testing scenario than from a solution that's fully implemented. Learn what's good about your prototypes and what doesn't work. Just as you did in your brainstorming session, combine the best elements of different prototypes if you can. After evaluating the results of your tests you'll arrive at the best solution.

IMPLEMENTING Once you've learned all there is to learn from testing your promising prototypes, it's time to put the best ideas into action. It isn't always as easy as it sounds. Depending on the scale of changes you're making, a lot of planning might need to happen. You might need to educate staff, or you might need to do some construction. The important thing is that everyone is on the same page and works together to make the implementation a success. This will be much easier to do if your design process has been inclusive all along, so be sure to get folks involved from the start.

Design Everything

Our definition of design is so broad because this process can be applied any time you're creating anything. For instance, the authors of Cook's Illustrated use this process to write their recipes. They often start by observing a problem ("Tuna salad is usually too watery") and brainstorming methods for improvement ("Pat the tuna with kitchen towels? Put it in a colander?"), and then they create the dish with their new methods. The recipe goes through many iterations as they find out which methods successfully solve the problem and which don't. How do they know whether something's making an improvement? They test the recipe by eating the dish. Finally, the recipe is implemented when it appears in their publication.

So. Libraries and everything in them can be designed. The best thing about this is how liberating it is. We're all designers, and we don't have to wait for some creative genius to improve our libraries. We have a method to employ when we need to improve and innovate. Now get out there and do it!

Design everything?
While everything *can* be designed, not every little decision needs to go through a full-blown design process. Clearly, you'd never accomplish anything if you conducted user interviews every time you needed to create a new bookmark. That being said, there's little doubt that your bookmarks would benefit from review by some staff or a library member to see if they need a revision or two. In the end, all you need to do is use your best judgment about how much time a product should spend in the design process.

9.3 Your Organizational Culture

If you've read this far into the book, we're guessing that you're well convinced of the validity *and* viability of the user experience framework to make positive changes in our libraries. We're truly thrilled about that! However, the very last thing we want to do is get you excited about these techniques and ideas and send you on your way to implementing them without spending a bit of time discussing some of the organizational challenges around implementation and how you might overcome them.

The bottom line? You won't be able to implement any of the ideas in this book without the right organizational culture. What's the right organizational culture? It's a culture that puts the user first at every level, starting with full support from senior administration, all the way down to complete buy-in at the grassroots level. How do you develop that culture? We have a few ideas.

Develop Mission and Vision Statements Together

In checkpoint 5.1, we talked about the importance of having a service philosophy and developing that service philosophy with involvement of all service staff. Whereas a service philosophy acts as a guide for your service desk staff, mission and vision statements should act as guides for everything you do at your library. Your mission statement enshrines what you do now. Your vision statement should be aspirational, giving you, as an organization, something to aim for. Make sure you develop both statements with your staff to get their buy-in, and also make sure that your statements have your members at their core. If you already have a mission and a vision, maybe now is a good time to review them with your staff, once again making sure that the organizational goal of an outstanding user experience is at the heart of those statements.

Don't Be Afraid to Evangelize

One of the best library website redesign stories we've heard starts with a UX-loving web librarian who assembled a redesign project team and, at the first meeting of the team, distributed copies of Steve Krug's *Don't Make Me Think* to every member of the team. Why was that such a good idea? If you've read Krug's book, you know that his easy, no-nonsense approach puts the user at the center of all web development decisions, which was exactly the reason why our UX-loving web librarian gave the team members their own copies of the book. He wanted to ensure that each of them set aside their own personal stakes in the website redesign and to get them all in the right mindset to develop a truly user-centered website.

We like that example because it highlights the importance of evangelizing good ideas. We don't assume that everyone works in organizations where every staff member automatically puts the user first in everything they do. In fact, we assume that most people *don't* work in organizations like that, not because we assume most organizations are bad, but simply because we know that in our day-to-day jobs, it can be easy to get bogged down in tasks and deadlines and forget that the reason we do what we do is to make our members' lives better. We all need that little reminder every once in a while. So, like the example of the web development librarian above, we say don't be afraid to share your love of UX. The next time you read a great article or book about UX design, tell your colleagues about it. The next time you hear a great conference speaker talking about how UX can improve the way you do what you do, invite her to speak at your staff day. The best way to get your colleagues on board is to expose them to the ideas that got you fired up in the first place.

Lobby for UX Staff

Whether or not you are on the management team at your library (where you probably have some leverage when it comes to proposing new positions), we say go ahead and lobby for a UX librarian or two at your library. Having a dedicated staff member or team is ideal because it means one person or team is responsible for overseeing all aspects of the library's user experience.

If fiscal times are particularly tough and it's unlikely that your organization will be able to support a staff member or team devoted to UX, consider setting up a cross-departmental committee that will come together to focus on assessing and improving the library's UX. And whereas having a full-time staff member devoted to the task is preferable (since a committee is usually just an additional responsibility piled on to already full-time workloads), sometimes a committee is all your library can afford, and that might be fine, especially if your library is only just getting into UX work. Try to gather folks who are truly passionate about improving the user experience at your library and give them the tools and authority to make changes. Whether it's a staff member, team, or committee, just having *someone* to push through UX work is crucial because every idea needs a champion to really fly.

Recruit Staff to Help with User Research

If you've done any usability testing at all, you know how powerful and enlightening it can be to watch someone struggle to accomplish something on a website that makes complete sense to you. It's for the same reason that we usually recommend recruiting staff members from across the organization, including folks from the front lines as well as senior management, to help with any user research efforts you have planned. There is no greater endorsement for UX principles and methods than, for example, doing a user observation exercise in the lobby of your library and seeing your members struggle to find their way around. And when you involve staff members as well as management, you can almost hear the "aha!" moments dawn on them as they undertake the observation exercises. Their involvement will help sell UX concepts, principles, and methods to them, resulting in buy-in from frontline staff and endorsement from management.

Good UX and Innovation Aren't at Odds

We once knew of a librarian (who shall remain nameless) who went on a multi-year diatribe against UX principles and methods, claiming that UX is incremental and reactionary and doesn't really allow a library to innovate. If you come face-to-face with a similar complaint at your library, first take a deep breath, then calmly explain to your complainant that such an idea really is based on a misunderstanding of UX principles. If UX was all about *asking* users what would make their lives easier, then certainly, one could argue that innovation couldn't follow from such a practice. But since UX is really all about *understanding user behaviors* (as opposed to opinions), there is no reason why you couldn't dream up innovative solutions to user problems.

Organizational Needs Don't Have to Suffer

When we teach workshops on UX design for library websites, one of the most common questions we get asked is about where to put library policies on the website. The question usually goes something like this: "My administration is forcing me to put our policies on the website. I know our users don't care about policies. What do I do?" While your particular issue might not be where to put the library's policies on your website, you might face similar tensions between what's good for the library versus what's good for the user.

> ### Organizational culture, UX, and criticism
>
> It is impossible to improve your library's UX without being critical. There's no getting around it. But being critical does *not* mean you have to be negative. Good thing, because being negative about people's work is a surefire way to get everyone in your library to hate UX efforts, which will leave you feeling isolated and result in zero buy-in for UX at your library.
>
> Instead of emphasizing why a certain touchpoint needs drastic improvement, focus on the opportunities at hand. Illustrate how a touchpoint can be improved to better meet the needs of library members. Inevitably, part of this process involves pointing out how current solutions are lacking, but keeping the focus on library members, not on your opinions, is a great way to make sure everyone is on the same page and that no one takes offense.

To address this tension, we usually turn to Jesse James Garrett, one of the godfathers of user experience design. In his seminal work, *The Elements of User Experience*, Garrett notes that user needs are just one element that goes into the development of the end product—other elements include things like business needs (or library needs), functional requirements (like features), and content requirements, among other things. All of which is to say that we are not naive in believing that the only element we have to consider when designing things (websites, spaces, interfaces, service desks, *anything*) for our libraries is user needs; there are a lot of other elements we need to consider as well.

So to the poor web librarian who is struggling with the issue of library policies, we usually say this: Indeed, most of your users don't care about your policies, but the fact of the matter is, your library cares. It's a business need of yours, so don't fight it. In this example, the difference between a user-centered library and one that is not is that the former would find a low-trafficked, low-profile place for those policies (for example, by putting the link to library policies in the footer) and the latter would feature those policies prominently in its main navigation area. Act accordingly.

9.4 **Parting Words**

Well, this is good-bye! Thanks for reading.

We'll leave you with a final thought that we think sums up what this book has been all about:

> *Every decision we make affects how people experience the library.*
> *Let's make sure we're creating improvements.*

Happy designing,
Amanda and Aaron

appendix

Keeping Score

Here are all the checkpoints from this book at a glance, with a space to record your scores. After you've assessed everything, use one of the charts that follows to plot your scores.

Physical Space (see chapter 3)	
The library building is clean and functions as intended	/ 25
The library building is free from clutter	/ 20
Furniture adequately supports member needs	/ 20
The building supports diverse behaviors	/ 20
Members have easy access to power outlets	/ 15
Total for Physical Space	/ 100

Service Points (see chapter 4)	
Members readily approach service desks	/ 25
Service desks adjust to changing needs	/ 25
Members receive assistance when and where they need it	/ 25
Members receive the kind of assistance they need	/ 25
Total for Service Points	/ 100

Policies and Customer Service (see chapter 5)

Your library has a service philosophy	/ 10
Your staff members know and live your service philosophy	/ 15
There is as little policy as possible	/ 15
Library policies empower staff	/ 20
Staff members are friendly and genuinely want to help	/ 15
Service is consistent across departments and modalities	/ 10
Service is consistent across the organization	/ 15
Total for Policies and Customer Service	/ 100

Signage and Wayfinding (see chapter 6)

Your library has a brand manual that is consistent with the principles of graphic design	/ 25
All signage uses the same visual language	/ 15
Different types of signs are visually distinct	/ 10
There are as few signs as possible	/ 10
There are no paper signs taped to walls, doors, tables, computers, or any other surfaces	/ 10
Regulatory signs are written in a plain, polite, and friendly manner	/ 10
Library cards contain useful information and employ the library's visual language	/ 5
First-time visitors can easily locate all parts of the library	/ 15
Total for Signage and Wayfinding	/ 100

Online Presence (see chapter 7)	
Members can easily search for library items and place holds	/ 10
Members can easily accomplish critical tasks	/ 20
The size of your website is commensurate with the amount of effort you can devote to it	/ 10
Web content is engaging	/ 10
Content is written for the web	/ 10
Website employs web design conventions	/ 10
Home page clearly expresses what people can do on your site	/ 10
Website is easy to use on all devices	/ 10
Website employs the library's visual language	/ 5
You use social media tools in meaningful ways	/ 5
Total for Online Presence	/ 100

Using the Library (see chapter 8)	
The technology in your library is relevant, useful, and usable	/ 25
Collections are relevant to member needs	/ 15
Marketing materials are relevant to member needs	/ 10
You merchandize your materials	/ 20
Library services and programs solve problems	/ 30
Total for Using the Library	/ 100

Using one of these blank radar charts, write the name of one of the six categories from the preceding table at each corner. Then mark your total score with a dot on each corresponding line. Connect the dots. This will give you a graphical representation of your UX strengths and what needs to be improved.

There are a few blank charts here, so you can reassess and record your progress over time.

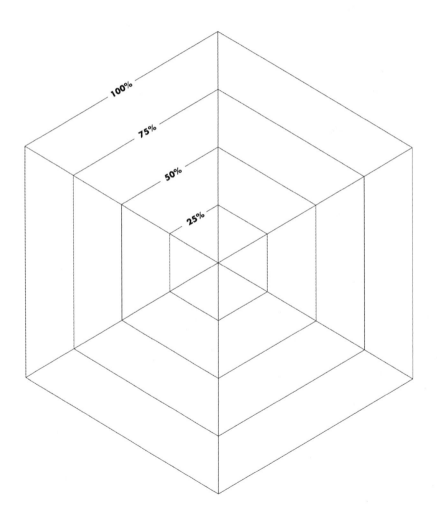

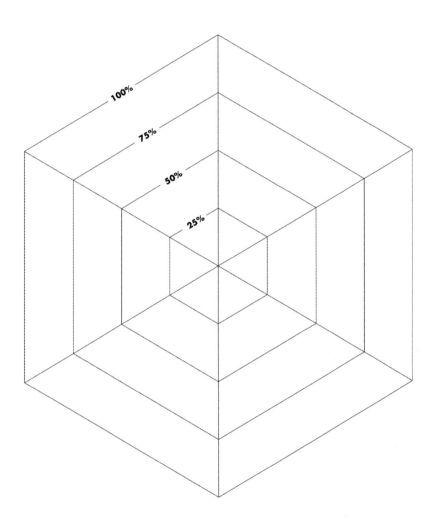

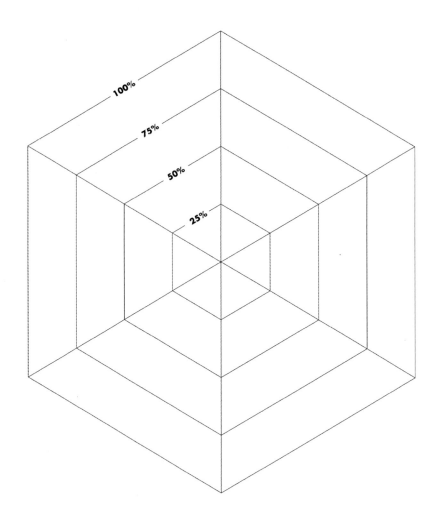

index